A Short History
of Congregational Singing

Cliff Ganus

Congrational Singing Press
Searcy, Arkansas
www.congregationalsinging.com

This book is dedicated to
Debbie Ganus
a singer and worshipper
who has shared and enriched my life

CONTENTS

PREFACE ix

CHAPTER 1. SINGING IN THE EARLY CHURCH 1
  Beyond Judea 1
  When they sang 2
  General characteristics of early Christian singing 4

CHAPTER 2. SOME EARLY CHRISTIAN SONGS 11
  Greek songs 13
  The earliest surviving piece of Christian music....................15
  The Odes of Solomon 17
  Characteristics of early church songs 18

CHAPTER 3. LEGALIZATION AND ESTABLISHMENT 19
  Constantine 20
  Congregational participation declines....................................22
  Early Latin Hymns 23
  Augustine 26
  The Medieval Period..27
  Corolingian influence..28

CHAPTER 4. REFORMATION HYMNODY AND PIETISM 31
  Jan Hus..31
  Martin Luther 32
  German congregational singing after Luther 39
  Pietism..40
  Zwingli and the Anabaptists..43
  The expanding reach of song 46

CHAPTER 5. REFORMATION PSALMODY 47
  Jean Calvin..47
  Henry VIII and the Anglican Church..51
  Sternhold and Hopkins...53
  The Scottish Psalter...58
  Other English psalters 59

CHAPTER 6. SEVENTEENTH-CENTURY PSALMODY 63
  The New Version...66
  American psalmody 70

CHAPTER 7. EARLY BRITISH HYMNODY 75
  Beginnings of English hymnody...75
  Isaac Watts 78

CHAPTER 8. THE WESLEYS AND THEIR SUCCESSORS....................87
  The Wesleys 88
  George Whitefield 98
  Later hymnody 98
  The Olney Hymns 100

CHAPTER 9. SINGING SCHOOLS AND EARLY AMERICAN HYMNODY 105
  Billings and fuging tunes 107
  American hymnody..109
  The Great Revival and camp meeting songs.......................................109
  The Sacred Harp 112
  Lowell Mason 113
  Organs, choirs, Campbellites, Shakers, and Mormons 114

CHAPTER 10. DEVELOPMENTS IN BRITISH HYMNODY 117
  An authorized hymnal...118
  The Oxford Movement 120
  Twentieth-century hymnals..124

CHAPTER 11. GOSPEL AND CONVENTION SONGS...........................127
  Gospel songs 127
  Songs and evangelism...128
  Other gospel song writers 130
  Convention songs..132

CHAPTER 12. CONTINUITY AND CHANGE 135
  Gospel music and spirituals 136
  Commercialism and Christian music 137
  Iconoclasts, worship wars, and the New Wave 138
  Worship renewal 140

CHAPTER 13. THE FUTURE OF CONGREGATIONAL SINGING 143
  Why do we sing? 143
  The role of music 145
  Two ironies 146
  Instrumental music and musical style 147
  Reconsidering the texts 149
  The story continues 150

APPENDIX 1. WHAT HAPPENS IN THE CONGREGATION 153
  Meetings in the early church and today 153
  The Christian's audience 156

APPENDIX 2. CEREMONY AND SERVICE 159

SELECTIVE BIBLIOGRAPHY 165

INDEX 169

PREFACE

The emergence of hymnology, or the study of congregational singing, as a legitimate topic for investigation was marked by the publication of John Julian's monumental *A Dictionary of Hymnology* in 1892. Subsequently, many authors have explored how hymns represent the people and circumstances that produced them along with their impact on spiritual development, community, and evangelism.

This short book, designed to be used as a text in my hymnology classes at Harding University, is in that tradition. It is not a history of church music. Its subject consists of songs intended to be sung by congregations rather than performed by choirs or by trained musicians. Rather than being a collection of hymn stories, it describes the settings behind those stories. Throughout the book I have tracked important events and ideas in order to provide a sense of the environment in the church's history that produced its songs. The purposes are to introduce readers to that rich and varied heritage that forms the bedrock of our congregational singing; to trace recent developments; and to encourage thoughtful contemplation and discussion regarding the nature and future of church music. There are deliberate efforts to ascertain the function and importance of congregational singing in church meetings in the church's infancy, throughout its history, and in the present. This book essentially tells the history of all of us who sing congregationally today, since our present practices have been shaped by those who preceded us.

To encourage a fresh hearing of texts and an appreciation for their original settings, I have made a deliberate attempt to pair hymns with contemporaneous tunes. For example, when we discuss Isaac Watts' 1707 poem "Alas! and Did My Savior Bleed?" we will not show it with the commonly used 1885 musical setting by Ralph E. Hudson, with its anachronistic refrain. It is instead presented with a tune that Watts would have known and might have sung with his own congregation in London. The intent is to place texts and tunes together as they might have originally been heard in the hope that this will lead to a fresh hearing.

I have devoted extra attention to Luther, Calvin, Watts, and the Wesleys because of their reputation during their lifetime and the influence they have exerted on congregational song.

Throughout these pages there are references to song numbers in *Praise for the Lord*[1] (designated PftL), a hymnal with a slight ecumenical flavor but primarily designed for Churches of Christ. Keying the book to this hymnal has influenced, though not dictated, which hymns would be considered for discussion.

I am indebted to Drs. Michael Claxton, Randy Gill, and Dennis Organ for their friendship and for their generous participation in reading drafts of this text and offering valuable suggestions.

Cliff Ganus
April 2021

---

[1] *Praise for the Lord*, ed. John P. Wiegand. Nashville: Praise Press, 1997.

CHAPTER 1

SINGING IN THE EARLY CHURCH

Although the Christian church that was established in Jerusalem around A.D. 30 was radically new at its core, culturally it was rooted in two thousand years of Jewish tradition. Converts to the movement continued to honor the book of Psalms, which played a significant role in Jewish home, temple, and synagogue life. They established their own synagogues; met in the temple court and in various houses to eat, pray, and discuss the teachings of the apostles;[1] and continued to be Jewish in ethnicity, culture, practice, tradition, and most religious celebrations. Their music featured modal melodies and vocal ornamentation similar to those of their Arabic neighbors, the echoes of which we still hear today in minaret calls and synagogue chants.

Jews placed a high value on their ancient beliefs, traditions, and ceremonies; and the Roman government, which respected antiquity, allowed Israel to continue to live and worship as they had long before Rome was established and to be exempt from observing Roman religious rituals. For its first three decades the Christian church was granted the same dispensation, since the Roman authorities viewed it as a Jewish sect.

Beyond Judea

Alexander the Great (356-323 B.C.E.) had spread Greek culture as far eastward as India, and the Greek language was established as the language of diplomacy and of the educated in the Macedonian Empire and its successors. Thus, as the apostle Paul and other evangelists took the good news outside of Judea, they spoke and wrote in Greek, the *lingua franca* of the eastern Roman Empire.

---

[1] Acts 2:42-47

However, the Hellenistic influence did not replace foundational culture, and as churches were planted they were each shaped by local social practices, musical styles, philosophies, and religious customs. Churches in different locations varied in their meeting times, their music, their language, and the format of their meetings. They had different understandings about leadership, about the role of women in the church, about the relationship of the body and the spirit, and about doctrinal issues. There was no common hymnal and no repertoire of familiar traditional church songs. Christians who traveled from their home area to other parts of the Roman world would find churches that looked and sounded quite different from the ones that they had left.

One of the common assumptions in this ancient world was that music held remarkably powerful qualities. Stories were told of Orpheus, whose singing could affect animals, divert the course of streams, charm rocks and trees, and exercise remarkable control over people. Because of its powers, Aristotle and other philosophers taught that appropriate music should be at the core of a young man's education and that the type of music he heard would help to determine the sort of person he would become. Melodic declamation lifted poetry and drama to a status above that of ordinary speech, and important Jewish and pagan ceremonial texts were invariably sung rather than being merely spoken.

When they sang

The New Testament mentions singing in a few passages. Paul wrote to the church at Corinth, "How is it then, brethren? when ye come together, every one of you hath a psalm, hath a doctrine, hath a tongue, hath a revelation, hath an interpretation. Let all things be done unto edifying." (I Corinthians 14:26, KJV. Even though the NIV and other translations use the term "hymn" in this verse, the Greek word is *psalmos*.) Singing is implied in connection with the psalm, which would be melodiously intoned according to Jewish tradition. Although this is in a group setting, the text suggests individual rather than congregational presentation.

Paul's letters of Ephesians and Colossians also mention singing. To the Ephesians he writes, "Do not get drunk on wine, which leads to debauchery. Instead, be filled with the Spirit, speaking to one another with psalms, hymns, and songs from the Spirit.[2] Sing and make music from your heart to the Lord, always giving thanks to God the Father for everything, in the name of our Lord Jesus Christ...."[3] And to the Colossians: "Let the message of Christ dwell among you richly as you teach and admonish one another with all wisdom through psalms, hymns, and songs from the Spirit, singing to God with gratitude in your hearts."[4] There is no indication regarding whether this singing was done congregationally or individually.

It may be that the most important observation we can make of early Christian singing is that it was not restricted to an assembly. The combination of text and music produces a benefit that Paul recognizes as he writes, "Sing and make music from your heart to the Lord." Music connects head and heart, providing a way both to encourage and to express emotions.[5] And musical expressions of praise or of petition were important, whether the audience was God, those nearby, or one's self. James alludes to this when he writes, "Is any one of you in trouble? He should pray. Is anyone happy? Let him sing songs of praise."[6] There is no suggestion of postponing that prayer or praise until the next Sunday gathering.

The most significant example of the importance and role of singing to early Christians may be that of Paul and Silas in a Philippian prison, praying and singing songs of praise at midnight.[7] We might suppose that the two sang in Greek, rather than Hebrew, so they could be understood by their captive audience in this dark place. Singing was central to Christian life.

---

[2] "Songs from the Spirit," or "Spiritual songs," may refer to the ecstatic glossolalia described in I Corinthians 14:15: "I will sing with my spirit." Perhaps the term has a wider meaning.

[3] Ephesians 5:18-20

[4] Colossians 3:16

[5] Paul's comment in I Corinthians 14:15 invites clarification: "I will pray with my spirit, but I will also pray with my understanding; I will sing with my spirit, but I will also sing with my understanding." This passage is often cited as an exhortation to sing emotionally and fervently. However, Paul's discourse through this part of the chapter concerns glossolalia, or speaking, praying, and singing in tongues as guided by the spirit. Emotionally charged singing may have been, and presumably was, important to Paul and others. But that is not his point here.

[6] James 5:13. With "songs of praise" (Greek *psalleto*) James probably refers to the Hebrew psalms or similar texts of praise and gratitude.

[7] Acts 16:25

General characteristics of early Christian singing

Acts 16:25; I Corinthians 14:15, 26; Ephesians 5:18-20; Colossians 3:16; and James 5:13 are the only New Testament passages mentioning singing. Using a few other sources we can make the following observations.

1. The earliest singing of the church involved psalmody.

Singing in the temple was performed by designated Levites; in synagogues and homes more of the community would participate. Different circumstances required different modes of presentation. Responsorial psalmody occurs when a cantor recites a verse and the congregation or choir responds with a simple refrain, such as "For his mercy endures forever" or "Alleluia." In antiphonal psalmody, two groups recite alternately, a practice that was well suited to psalms in which verses consisted of two complementary phrases. An example of this "synonymous parallelism" can be found in Psalm 2, in which the second line of each pair repeats the idea expressed in the first:

> *Why do the nations conspire*
> *   and the peoples plot in vain?*
> *The kings of the earth take their stand*
> *   and the rulers gather together*
> *against the Lord*
> *   and against his Anointed One.*
> *"Let us break their chains," they say,*
> *   "and throw off their fetters."* (Psalm 2:1-3)

In the Jewish tradition different types of melodies would have been used, depending on whether the text was from the Psalms, the Law, the Prophets, or the Wisdom Literature. All of these styles were fairly simple, usually assigning one note to each syllable in the text, with occasional melodic decorations. Ornamentations were used to decorate important words or ideas. When rabbis or cantors prayed, the music tended to be more passionate, depending on the verbal content. These styles were probably carried over into practices of some congregations of the early church, especially those with a strong Jewish affiliation.

2. Early Christians lived in cultures that expected important texts to be sung, not simply spoken.

The epics of Homer and the poems of Sappho were sung to simple melodic formulas; to simply speak them would be to deny them the richness they deserved. Likewise, actors in Grecian and Roman theaters would be expected to chant their lines to tunes, accompanied by a group of instrumentalists who sat in the *orchestra*, the rounded area in front of the stage. We have extant fragments from Euripides' *Oresteia* including tunes that may have been written by the author himself.

In the Jewish tradition, the Babylonian Talmud (ca. A.D. 500) requires that scripture be read with "tunefulness," describing a long-established practice. It is interesting to imagine the scene recounted in Luke 4:16ff, where Jesus was invited to speak to the synagogue in Nazareth. He stood to read from Isaiah 61, and he would have chanted the scripture melodically. After reading, he rolled up the scroll, gave it to the attendant, sat down, and spoke to the congregation about the scripture's meaning.

Had Jesus not stood when reading the scripture, he would have shown disrespect. Had he simply spoken the scripture in conversational fashion without chanting it, he would have shown disrespect.

This cultural tradition extended to the early church. When a member or a congregation recited a text of praise, melodic declamation was expected.. Let's suppose that a leader of the church in Philippi was asked to read Paul's epistle to the congregation. When he came to the section which we call the Christ Hymn (Phil. 2:6-11), he might well have recognized the poetical structure and sung, not spoken, the text:

> *Who, being in very nature God,*
> *did not consider equality with God something to be grasped,*
> *but made himself nothing,*
> *taking the very nature of a servant,*
> *being made in human likeness.*
> *And being found in appearance as a man, he humbled himself*
> *and became obedient to death — even death on a cross!*
> *Therefore God exalted him to the highest place*
> *and gave him the name that is above every name,*
> *that at the name of Jesus every knee should bow,*
> *in heaven and on earth and under the earth,*
> *and every tongue confess that Jesus Christ is Lord,*
> *to the glory of God the Father.*

3. **The music of the early church was vocal and not instrumental**.
Early Christians with Jewish roots continued to participate in temple services in Jerusalem. Priestly instrumentalists and singers took part in

the temple liturgy, without the double pipes, drums, female musicians, or dancers which pagan ceremonies exploited for their emotional impact.

However, instruments were not used in early Christian assemblies. This was not a point of contention; the absence of instruments was not argued or explained in the New Testament scriptures. It was not until the end of the second century that Christian writers such as Clement of Alexandria[8] began to inveigh against the use of instruments to accompany praise. From this absence of earlier corrective teachings we assume that there had been no serious attempt to introduce them, perhaps for these reasons:

•Instruments were unnecessary and irrelevant for the purposes of reciting Christian texts. Instruments were associated with bards or performers, not community members.

•Early Christian practices echoed those of the synagogue rather than those of the temple. Temple instruments (especially shofars, drums, and trumpets) had signaling as well as musical functions, and some believe that one of the purposes of instruments in pagan and Jewish ceremonies was to mask the sounds of the sacrifices. Synagogue gatherings, which originated after the destruction of Solomon's temple, were more intimate and less ceremonial than the rites of Solomon's temple and used no instruments.

•Instruments were associated with pagan cults, and their role in those cults was often an important one. During the third century church fathers began prohibiting the use of the aulos, the lyre, the kithara, the sistrum, or the drum in Christian gatherings, because the use of these instruments carried connotations of pagan society.

4. **Early music was monophonic**.

Singing in all of the ancient world was monophonic, consisting of a single tune with no harmony,[9] Monophony would continue be the mode of performance for nearly a thousand years; in the Middle East and Asia, that tradition continued even longer.

There is no description or example of multiple-part music until the ninth century; poetic rhyme comes from the eleventh century; and the Renaissance gave us the first sampling of what would sound to us today like congregational singing in a church.

---

[8] c.150-c.215; *The Instructor*, Book II, Chapter IV

[9] This is essentially true, though drones and heterophony might have been employed..

5. **There was not a common repertoire of hymns**.
Jewish Christians were familiar with the psalms, though complete psalters were expensive and relatively rare. As the church spread, diverse traditions produced other songs. Christians in Ephesus, for example, probably sang hymns to Christ that had formerly been sung to Diana. Hymns that were well received might be carried to different locations as church members and leaders traveled.

6. **Singing in the assembly was done by individuals and perhaps by congregations**.
There was a tradition of group singing in Greece, as documented by Xenophon, writing around 360 B.C.: "When the tables had been removed and the guests had poured a libation and sung a hymn, there entered a man from Syracuse, to give them an evening's merriment."[10] But there is no clear mention of group singing in the earliest church.

A possible reference to a congregational hymn comes at the beginning of the second century in Pliny's letter to the Emperor Trajan (ca. 112). In his investigation of a group of Christians, he had discovered that "they had been in the habit of meeting together on a stated day, before sunrise, and of offering in turns a form of invocation to Christ, as to a god; also of binding themselves by an oath, not for any guilty purpose, but not to commit thefts, or robberies, or adulteries, not to break their word, not to repudiate deposits when called upon; these ceremonies having been gone through, they had been in the habit of separating, and again meeting together for the purpose of taking food — food, that is, of an ordinary and innocent kind."[11]

7. **Congregational singing was apparently not central to early church meetings.**
In the few New Testament references to assemblies, the emphases are on fellowship, breaking bread (including the Lord's supper), teaching, prayer, edification, and encouragement. No document indicates that singing played a significant part in their meetings. We don't know when or if a common repertoire of hymns developed in the early church.

---

[10] Xenophon, *Symposium 2*

[11] John Delaware Lewis, *The Letters of the Younger Pliny, Literally Translated* (London: Trübner & Co., 1879), Book X, 378.

The Christian instructional manual called the *Didache*, composed around A.D. 100, issues rules concerning the assembly and practices of the church but does not mention singing.

Justin Martyr's account of a mid-second-century Christian meeting mentions readings, exhortation, praying, and the Lord's Supper — but not hymnody or psalmody:[12]

And we afterwards continually remind each other of these things. And the wealthy among us help the needy; and we always keep together; and for all things wherewith we are supplied, we bless the Maker of all through His Son Jesus Christ, and through the Holy Ghost. And on the day called Sunday, all who live in cities or in the country gather together to one place, and the memoirs of the apostles or the writings of the prophets are read, as long as time permits; then, when the reader has ceased, the president verbally instructs, and exhorts to the imitation of these good things. Then we all rise together and pray, and, as we before said, when our prayer is ended, bread and wine and water are brought, and the president in like manner offers prayers and thanksgivings, according to his ability, and the people assent, saying Amen; and there is a distribution to each, and a participation of that over which thanks have been given, and to those who are absent a portion is sent by the deacons. And they who are well to do, and willing, give what each thinks fit; and what is collected is deposited with the president, who succours the orphans and widows and those who, through sickness or any other cause, are in want, and those who are in bonds and the strangers sojourning among us, and in a word takes care of all who are in need. But Sunday is the day on which we all hold our common assembly, because it is the first day on which God, having wrought a change in the darkness and matter, made the world; and Jesus Christ our Saviour on the same day rose from the dead. For He was crucified on the day before that of Saturn (Saturday); and on the day after that of Saturn, which is the day of the Sun, having appeared to His apostles and disciples, He taught them these things, which we have submitted to you also for your consideration.

---

[12] *Apology 1*, 67

CHAPTER 2

SOME EARLY CHRISTIAN SONGS

A few early Christian hymns are available to us, having been of such significance that they were preserved in manuscripts. The New Testament includes three canticles[1] recorded in Luke's gospel. First among these is Mary's song, known as the Magnificat, because of its first word in Latin.

My soul glorifies the Lord
  and my spirit rejoices in God my Savior,
for he has been mindful
  of the humble state of his servant.
From now on all generations will call me blessed,
  for the Mighty One has done great things for me — holy is his name.
His mercy extends to those who fear him,
  from generation to generation.
He has performed mighty deeds with his arm;
  he has scattered those who are proud in their inmost thoughts.
He has brought down rulers from their thrones
  but has lifted up the humble.
He has filled the hungry with good things
  but has sent the rich away empty.
He has helped his servant Israel,
  remembering to be merciful
to Abraham and his descendants forever,
  even as he said to our fathers. (Luke 1:46b-55)

The second of these is Zechariah's song[2] on the birth of John the Baptist.

Praise be to the Lord, the God of Israel,
  because he has come and has redeemed his people.

---

[1] A canticle is a poetical text taken from scripture, excluding the Psalms. A number of canticles have been specifically designated for use in Catholic and Orthodox liturgies.

[2] known as the *Benedictus Dominus*, after the Latin incipit

He has raised up a horn of salvation for us
  in the house of his servant David
  (as he said through his holy prophets of long ago),
salvation from our enemies
  and from the hand of all who hate us —
to show mercy to our fathers
  and to remember his holy covenant,
the oath he swore to our father Abraham:
to rescue us from the hand of our enemies,
  and to enable us to serve him without fear
in holiness and righteousness before him all our days.
And you, my child, will be called a prophet of the Most High;
  for you will go on before the Lord to prepare the way for him,
to give his people the knowledge of salvation
  through the forgiveness of their sins,
because of the tender mercy of our God,
  by which the rising sun will come to us from heaven
to shine on those living in darkness and in the shadow of death,
  to guide our feet into the path of peace. (Luke 1:68-79)

And the third is the song of Simeon's upon his encounter with the infant
Jesus in the temple.[3]

Sovereign Lord, as you have promised,
  you now dismiss your servant in peace.
For my eyes have seen your salvation,
  which you have prepared in the sight of all people,
a light for revelation to the Gentiles
  and for glory to your people Israel. (Luke 2:29-31)

By including these three texts, clearly in the style of Hebrew poetry, in
his letter to Theophilus, Luke attests to the Jewish roots of the Christian
church, while Simeon's song announces the inclusion of the Gentiles
among those whom the child's ministry will bless.

In Ephesians 5:14, Paul uses an introductory formula to indicate that the
short baptismal formula he is quoting is already known:

for it is light that makes everything visible. This is why it is said:
  "Wake up, O sleeper,
  rise from the dead,
  and Christ will shine on you."

---

[3] or *Nunc dimittis*

This text was probably chanted by congregations as initiates rose from their baptismal waters. Had he not used the words "This is why it is said," we might have supposed that Paul was the author of the text; by using that introduction he assures us that it is already public property.

Likewise, in his second letter to Timothy, Paul indicates that the magnificent text citing the faithfulness of God is already familiar to his readers:

Here is a trustworthy saying:
If we died with him,
* we will also live with him;*
if we endure,
* we will also reign with him.*
If we disown him,
* he will also disown us;*
if we are faithless,
* he will remain faithful,*
* for he cannot disown himself.* (II Timothy 2:11-13)

We have already observed the Christ-hymn of Philippians 2:6-11. A shorter example is found in I Timothy 3:16:

Beyond all question, the mystery of godliness is great:
He appeared in a body,
* was vindicated by the Spirit,*
was seen by angels,
* was preached among the nations,*
was believed on in the world,
* was taken up in glory.*

John's Revelation also contains hymns which may have become familiar in different locales by the time that he wrote, in 4:11; 5:9-10,12,13; 11:15,17-18; 15:3-4; and 19:5,6.

Greek songs

The hymns found in the epistles and in Revelation do not reflect a Jewish tradition. Jewish influence faded as the church spread geographically and declined dramatically after the fall of Jerusalem and the destruction of the temple in A.D. 70 and a subsequent razing of the city in A.D. 135. During the next two centuries, Greek was the dominant church language, and a number of hymns from this period survive.

This hymn was written by Clement (c.170-c.220), the headmaster for a dozen years of the Catechetical School of Alexandria and possibly a teacher of the church historian Origen. It uses a percussive poetical style, with short, colorful phrases, incorporating a variety of metaphorical images:

> *Bridle of untamed colts, Wing of unwandering birds, Sure helm of ships, Shepherd of royal lambs.*
>
> *Assemble thy simple children to praise holily, to hymn guilelessly with innocent mouths,*
>
> *Christ the guide of children. O King of Saints, all-subduing Word of the most high Father, Ruler of Wisdom, Support of sorrows, rejoicing in eternity,*
>
> *Jesus, Savior of the human race, Shepherd, Husbandman, Helm, Bridle, Heavenly Wing of the all-holy flock, Fisher of men who are saved, catching the chaste fishes with sweet life from the hateful wave of a sea of vices —*
>
> *Guide us, Shepherd of rational sheep; guide, O holy King, thy children safely along the footsteps of Christ; O heavenly Way, perennial Word, immeasurable Age, eternal Light, Fount of mercy, Performer of virtue; noble is the life of those who hymn God,*
>
> *O Christ Jesus, heavenly milk of the sweet breasts of the graces of the Bride, pressed out of Thy wisdom.*
>
> *Babes nourished with tender mouths, filled with the dewy spirit of the rational milk, let us sing together simple praises, true hymns to Christ our King, holy fee for the teaching of life; let us sing in simplicity the powerful Child.*
>
> *O choir of peace, the Christ-begotten, O chaste people, let us sing together the God of peace.*

Henry Dexter claimed that his "Shepherd of Tender Youth" (PftL 576) was based on Clement's text, though the relationship is a distant one.

Phos hilaron ("Joyful light"), sometimes known as the "Candlelighting Hymn," was associated with dusk, when lamps were lit. It may date back as far as the second century, since Basil (ca. 329-79) reported it as having a rich tradition extending long before his time.

> *Christ, gladdening light of holy glory,*
> *glory of God, heavenly Father immortal,*
> *the holy blessed one, our Lord Jesus Christ:*
> *we come now to the peaceful hour of sunset;*
> *we see the star of evening shine;*
> *we sing to the Father, the Son, and the Holy Spirit, one God.*
> *You are worthy at all times to be praised*
> *and honored with pure and pious songs,*
> *God's only Son, our only life-giver;*
> *wherefore all the world gives glory to you, its Master.*

Also from the third century is the Greek morning hymn now known as the "Gloria" (also called the "Greater Doxology"), again constructed of a series of short compelling phrases:

Glory in the heavens to God,
and on earth peace, to men, favor.
We praise you, we bless you,
we worship you, we give thanks to you,
on account of your great glory,
Lord, heavenly King, God the Father Almighty;
Lord, only Son, Jesus Christ; and Holy Spirit.
O Lord God, the Lamb of God, the Son of the Father,
you who take away the sins of the world, have mercy upon us;
you who take away the sins of the world, receive our petition;
you who sit on the right hand of the Father, have mercy on us.
Because you only are holy, you only are Lord, Jesus Christ,
unto the glory of God the Father. Amen.

The earliest surviving piece of Christian music

In 1918 a torn piece of papyrus was discovered in Oxyrhynchus, Egypt, with a fragment of a hymn text from the third century. A significant part of the text is missing; what is left translates like this:

All of God's wondrous works … nor let the bright glittering stars be silent …
all the rivers' resounding torrents; and while we sing … to Father and Son
and Holy Spirit let all the powers answer and shout aloud Amen! Amen! …
might and worship … the giver alone of all that is good. Amen! Amen!

The unique characteristic of this discovery is that accompanying the hymn text is Greek musical notation, showing the tune to which the hymn was sung. We do not know whether it was widely or locally distributed or if it was congregationally or individually sung; and, of course, a significant portion has been lost. Nevertheless, this is the only hymn fragment from the first few centuries that contains both words and music, and it provides a tantalizing insight into early hymnody. The fact that it was notated indicates a certain importance, perhaps by association with a Christian of some stature or because of some general familiarity or significance.

This conjectural completion of the hymn[4] was a project in a class taught by David H. Tripp, an instructor at Lincoln Theological College in

---

4 Tripp and Wheeler, "The Oldest Christian Hymn with Music," p. 24, reprinted with permission.

Oxyrhynchus hymn reconstruction

England in the 1980s. Bracketed notes and words have been supplied by the reconstruction team to replace those that are missing from the damaged manuscript. Singing this hymn today allows us to hear unique echoes of what some Chrstians sang seventeen centuries ago.

The Odes of Solomon

The Odes of Solomon, from an unknown author around the end of the first century, was originally written in either Syriac or Greek. In this pre-Nicene age, some detect Gnostic overtones in portions of the text. They have not been retained in church liturgy or in congregational hymnals. Here is Ode 16 (of 42 in the collection), translated by James Charlesworth.

As the occupation of the ploughman is the ploughshare, and the occupation of the helmsman is the steering of the ship, so also my occupation is the psalm of the Lord by His hymns.

My art and my service are in His hymns, because His love has nourished my heart, and His fruits He poured unto my lips.

For my love is the Lord; hence I will sing unto Him.

For I am strengthened by His praises, and I have faith in Him.

I will open my mouth, and His Spirit will speak through me the glory of the Lord and His beauty,

The work of His hands, and the labor of His fingers;

For the multitude of His mercies, and the strength of His Word.

For the Word of the Lord investigates that which is invisible, and reveals His thought.

For the eye sees His works, and the ear hears His thought.

It is He who made the earth broad, and placed the waters in the sea.

He expanded the heaven, and fixed the stars.

And He fixed the creation and set it up, then He rested from His works.

And created things run according to their courses, and work their works, for they can never cease nor fail.

And the hosts are subject to His Word.

The reservoir of light is the sun, and the reservoir of darkness is the night.

For He made the sun for the day so that it will be light; but night brings darkness over the face of the earth.

And by their portion one from another they complete the beauty of God.

And there is nothing outside of the Lord, because He was before anything came to be.

And the worlds are by His Word, and by the thought of His heart.

Praise and honor to His name.

Hallelujah.

Characteristics of early church songs

Some of these early songs, including the Lukan canticles, demonstrate an origin in Hebrew poetry, utilizing synonymous parallelism. The later Greek hymns, with a Hellenistic influence, share common characteristics:
• Most of these songs were literally "hymns" — songs of praise.[5]
•These hymns were filled with colorful imagery, expressed in a flurry of short, pointed phrases.
•As seen in the few pagan hymns extant with notated music and the Oxyrhynchus hymn, Greek hymns were sung to simple tunes, in syllabic style (with one note per syllable).

---

[5] A few Greek words are translated as "praise" or "worship" in modern translations. The most common is *proskuneo* ("to kiss toward"), which conveyed the image of a servant prostrating himself before his master in adoration, an important concept in the ancient world and in the early church. The word appears sixty times in the New Testament. Whereas Greek words such as *latreuo* or *leiturgia* relate to ceremony, obedience, service, or sacrifice, *proskuneo* refers solely to praise and adoration. It implies being in the presence of the one who is adored.

CHAPTER 3

LEGALIZATION AND ESTABLISHMENT

Through the second and third centuries, the church was affected by two powerful movements, one internal and one external. The first was the tendency toward centralization of power. During the first century, it appears that a plurality of bishops were appointed in each city, with presumably equal authority or influence; and congregations were considered relatively autonomous, especially after the disruption of the Jerusalem church in A.D. 70. Later, some bishops began to accrue power to claim sole authority over a given city or territory. Churches in these areas came to follow the practices, even the developing liturgies, of the bishop's church. By the late third century a few groups met in newly constructed buildings accommodating fifty or sixty people rather than in homes.[1]

The second change had to do with increased political oppression of the church. As Christians abandoned the identity and practices of the Jewish community, they lost the religious exemptions granted to the Jewish nation. From the time of Nero (r. 54-68) the government had begun to look upon the church with suspicion, and it was he who, according to tradition, called for the executions of Paul and Peter. With Domitian (r. 81-96) the persecutions increased. During the next two centuries Roman leaders viewed the church with varying degrees of animosity, culminating in the Great Persecution of Diocletian (r. 284-305), who, beginning in 303, issued a series of decrees designed to force emperor worship on Christians.

The results were predictable. Many Christians were executed for refusing to comply. A few fled, and others in order to save their lives made the decision to deny their faith.[2] Claiming to be a follower of Jesus called for courage and commitment and was potentially fatal. Significantly, estimates

---

[1] Eusebius, *Ecclesiastical History* 8.1.5

[2] Later, their pleas to be readmitted to fellowship caused great difficulties.

of the numbers of Christians in the empire at that time range from five to twenty percent of the entire population.

Ironically, it was Diocletian's successor, Constantine, who became the Christian church's greatest friend — or its most unfortunate benefactor, depending on one's interpretation of history.

Constantine

Constantine's early connections with Christianity are uncertain; he claimed to have seen the symbol of Christ (the Greek letters *chi* and *rho*) in the sky before the battle in which he won control of the western portion of the empire. In 313 he and Licinius issued the Edict of Milan, which, among other things, legalized Christianity, returned Christians' confiscated property, and authorized Sunday as a day of worship.

Constantine was not devoutly or exclusively a Christian practitioner. He continued to promote the ancient pagan associations of the empire, he ordered the execution of a number of people (including a son and a wife), and he was not baptized until shortly before his death, at age sixty-five. But he showed interest in promoting and strengthening this religion under whose god he had won victories. Among other things, he recognized a particular threat in the teachings of Arius of Alexandria, who had proclaimed that Jesus was of a lower rank than God and that the Holy Spirit was lower yet. Although excommunicated by Bishop Alexander of Alexandria, Arius continued to preach his doctrine and to gain followers.

Constantine was no more than a dabbler in doctrine; his concern about Arianism was that it caused dissension in a group that formed a significant portion of his population. After defeating Licinius and becoming the ruler of the entire empire, he called a council of church leaders to meet in Nicaea in 325 to address the problem. He presided at the conference and perhaps wrote its report, which refuted Arius' doctrine, producing a creed that would provide a foundational statement for Christianity:

> *We believe in one God, the Father Almighty, maker of all things visible and invisible; and in one Lord Jesus Christ, the Son of God, the only-begotten of his Father, of the substance of the Father, God of God, Light of Light, very God of very God, begotten, not made, being of one substance with the Father. By whom all things were made, both which be in heaven and in earth. Who for us men and for our salvation came down and was incarnate and*

was made man. He suffered and the third day he rose again, and ascended into heaven. And he shall come again to judge both the quick and the dead. And in the Holy Ghost. And whosoever shall say that there was a time when the Son of God was not, or that before he was begotten he was not, or that he was made of things that were not, or that he is of a different substance or essence or that he is a creature, or subject to change or conversion — all that so say, the Catholic and Apostolic Church anathematizes them.

The concluding statement of condemnation was removed and minor changes were made at the Council of Constantinople in 381:

We believe in one God, the Father, the Almighty, maker of heaven and earth, of all that is, seen and unseen. We believe in one Lord, Jesus Christ, the only Son of God, eternally begotten of the Father, God from God, Light from Light, true God from true God, begotten, not made, of one Being with the Father. Through him all things were made. For us and for our salvation he came down from heaven: by the power of the Holy Spirit he became incarnate from the Virgin Mary, and was made man. For our sake he was crucified under Pontius Pilate; he suffered death and was buried. On the third day he rose again in accordance with the Scriptures; he ascended into heaven and is seated at the right hand of the Father. He will come again in glory to judge the living and the dead, and his kingdom will have no end.

We believe in the Holy Spirit, the Lord, the giver of life, who proceeds from the Father and the Son. With the Father and the Son he is worshiped and glorified. He has spoken through the Prophets. We believe in one holy catholic and apostolic Church. We acknowledge one baptism for the forgiveness of sins.

We look for the resurrection of the dead, and the life of the world to come. Amen.

The Council also fixed the date of Easter. But it was not successful in immediately eliminating Arianism, which was to cause significant disruption for the next half-century.

The Nicene Creed was not designed to be an obscure theological document. All Christians in the empire were expected to recite and subscribe to it. It is still spoken or sung, with slight alterations, in every Roman Catholic Mass. Christian songs often performed a didactic function as they were used to teach and to reinforce doctrine and to remind believers of the basic facts of their faith. Arius had also used hymns to promote his doctrines, but his works were suppressed, since he was the loser in the competition for orthodoxy, and are available only as reported by his opponents, notably Athanasius.[3]

What Constantine began by legalizing the church, Theodosius completed in a series of actions between 389 and 393, prohibiting pagan ceremonies (including what was left of the Olympic Games), allowing for the Christianizing of pagan sanctuaries, and requiring all church leaders to adhere to and proclaim the Trinitarian Nicene doctrine. Thus, in a remarkable reversal, the empire that had sought to destroy Christianity at the beginning of the fourth century had, by century's end, become history's first "Christian" nation!

Congregational participation declines

The fourth century was a period of great transition in the church, bringing changes in practically every area of its structure, practice, and role in society. Here are just a few of the results.

•Imposing buildings were constructed or repurposed to accommodate large groups. Constantine and his mother, Helen, built churches throughout the empire as monuments to sacred sites and events, including the first St. Peter's in Rome, marking the supposed location of Peter's grave. The Roman basilica plan became the standard for church buildings. The days of meeting in homes or in small rooms were gone.

•These meeting places were designated as holy sanctuaries, as had been the temples of previous Roman religions, and they were placed under the control of ordained clergy.

•The church became more politicized and hierarchal, since it was necessary in a theocracy for church and state to collaborate effectively. Church leaders were sometimes chosen more for their political acumen, wealth, or social status than for their spiritual qualities.

•Latin, the language of the government, became the standard language of the Western church.

•The confluence of the bishop-led fourth-century church and the priestly pagan cults led to the designation of certain ordained leaders to serve as intermediaries between man and God, and the role and participation of the ordinary Christian diminished. Non-ordained laymen were essentially

---

[3] For a discussion of his only surviving hymn, see Jonathan Hehn, "Congregational Song as Theological Debate in Late Antiquity: A Case Study of Arius's Thalia and the Development of Trinitarian Orthodoxy," *The Hymn*, Vol. 65, No. 1, Winter 2014, pp. 13-20.

spectators at religious events, and their responsibility to mutually encourage, instruct, and share received reduced emphasis.

As early evidence of these tidal changes in the church, consider the Council of Laodicea, held in the second half of fourth century. The delegates agreed on sixty "canons," or decrees. Here are three:

> *CANON XV. No others shall sing in the Church, save only the canonical singers, who go up into the ambo and sing from a book.*
>
> *CANON XXVIII. It is not permitted to hold love feasts, as they are called, in the Lord's Houses, or Churches, nor to eat and to spread couches in the house of God.*
>
> *CANON LIX. No psalms composed by private individuals nor any uncanonical books may be read in the church, but only the Canonical Books of the Old and New Testaments.[4]*

Here we see an intent to eliminate congregational singing; only those who have been specially trained and ordained were to participate. Also banned were love feasts, the fellowship meals that had been at the center of early Christian gatherings. Only the symbols of the wine and the host would be distributed, and the congregation was often forbidden to taste the wine. And hymns were abolished; only texts taken directly from scripture would be permissible. This final restriction was presumably to assure that no Arian or other heretical doctrine would be proclaimed in song.

The proclamations of the Laodicean synod were not immediately and universally obeyed, but they show the direction that the church was taking. Congregational participation in the church was in a significant decline.

Early Latin hymns

After Christianity became the recognized religion of the Empire, its documents and history were more carefully preserved, along with a number of hymns, some of which have been modified into forms suitable for placement in modern collections. The eastern portion of the church seemed to be more favorable to the inclusion of hymns into the liturgy. Hilary (ca. 300-68), Bishop of Poitiers, was exiled for a period of four years to Asia Minor, where he came into contact with eastern hymnody; he is often

---

[4] This regulation was designed to prevent heretical doctrines in the liturgy. There was no common scriptural canon until the fourth century. Athanasius was the first, in 367, to list the twenty-seven books still considered New Testament scripture.

credited with popularizing hymnody to the west upon his return. Some of his hymns are still sung.

Niceta of Remesiana (ca. 335-ca. 414) is considered by some to be the author of the *Te Deum*.[5]

We praise you O God,
we acknowledge you to be the Lord;
all the earth now worships you,
the Father everlasting.
To you all angels cry aloud,
the heavens and all the powers therein;
to you cherubim and seraphim continually do cry:
Holy, holy, holy
Holy Lord, God of Sabaoth,
heaven and earth are full of the majesty of your glory.
The glorious company
of the apostles praise you,
the goodly fellowship
of the prophets praise you,
the noble army of martyrs praise you,
the holy Church throughout all the world does acknowledge you:
the Father of an infinite majesty,
your adorable, true, and only Son,
also the Holy Spirit, the counselor.
You are the King of glory, O Christ.
You are the everlasting Son of the Father.
When you took upon yourself to deliver man,
you humbled yourself to be born of a virgin.
When you had overcome the sharpness of death,
you opened the kingdom
of heaven to all believers.
You sit at the right hand of God
in the glory of the Father.
We believe that you will come to be our judge.
We therefore pray you help your servants,
whom you have redeemed with your precious blood.
Make them to be numbered
with your saints in glory everlasting.
[6]*O Lord save your people*

---

[5] A more colorful legend has the *Te Deum* being improvised in antiphonal chant by Ambrose and Augustine when the former baptized the latter.

[6] The last thirteen lines, based on psalms, were added in later centuries.

and bless your heritage.
Govern them and lift them up forever.
Day by day we magnify you,
and we worship your name,
world without end.
Vouchsafe, O Lord,
to keep us this day without sin.
O Lord have mercy upon us, have mercy upon us.
O Lord, let your mercy be upon us,
as our trust is in you.
O Lord, in you have I trusted,
let me never be confounded.

Ambrose (ca. 340-97), who gained fame as a lawyer and provincial governor before being chosen bishop of Milan in 374, was to baptize Augustine
and to counsel Theodosius; he also wrote hymns. He received his bish-
opric during the continuing sputterings of the struggle against Arianism
and upheld the Nicene doctrine against powerful opponents when the
young Emperor Valentinian II and his mother, Justina, sought to designate
certain churches in Milan for Arian use. When the cathedral in Milan was
surrounded by Imperial troops demanding that Ambrose surrender it to
the Arians, Ambrose led his congregation in hymns within the cathedral,
loudly proclaiming their faith in the Father, Son, and Spirit. More than
a dozen extant hymns have been attributed to Ambrose (although their
authorship is ultimately uncertain), all in metrical unrhymed Latin poetry.
One of these is *Splendor paternae gloriae*, paired here, as it is commonly,
with a tune of later medieval vintage.

Splendor paternae gloriae

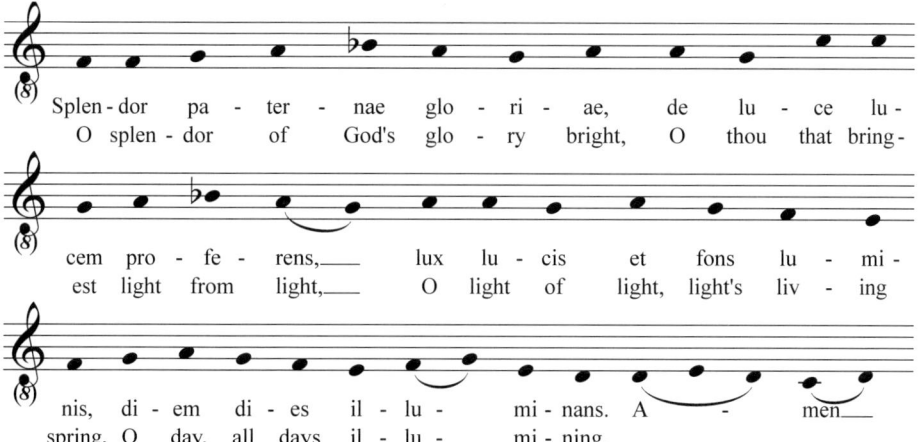

Aurelius Clemens Prudentius (348-413), a Spaniard, devoted the last part of his life to writing sacred verse; his *Corde natus ex parentis* (usually translated "Of the Father's Love Begotten") is still sung. Here is the first stanza, set to a thirteenth-century tune.

Of the Father's Love Begotten

Of the Fa-ther's love be - got - ten, Ere the worlds be - gan___ to be,

He is Al - pha and O - me - ga, He the source, the end - ding he,

Of the things that are, that have_____ been, And that fu - ture years

shall see, Ev - er-more and ev - er- more! A - men

Corde natus ex parentis
Ante mundi exordium
A et O cognominatus,
ipse fons et clausula
Omnium quae sunt, fuerunt,
quaeque post futura sunt.
Saeculorum saeculis.

Augustine

Though he wrote no hymns, Augustine (354-430), the Bishop of Hippo, in northern Africa, was influenced by them. In his *Confessions* he reflected over the power of hymnody and the relative roles of music and text:

> *At other times . . . I err in too great strictness; and sometimes to the degree as to wish the whole melody of sweet music which is used to David's Psalter, banished from my ears, and the Church's too; and that mode seems to me safer, which I remember to have been often told me of Athanasius, Bishop of*

*Alexandria, who made the reader of the psalm utter it with so slight inflec-
tion of voice, that it was nearer speaking than singing. Yet again, when I
remember the tears I shed at the Psalmody of Thy Church, in the beginning
of my recovered faith; and how at this time I am moved not with the singing,
but with the things sung, when they are sung with a clear voice and modu-
lation most suitable, I acknowledge the great use of this institution. Thus I
fluctuate between peril of pleasure and approved wholesomeness; inclined
the rather (though nor as pronouncing an irrevocable opinion) to approve
of the usage of singing in the church; that so by the delight of the ears the
weaker minds may rise to the feeding of devotion. Yet when it befalls me to
be more moved with the voice than the words sung, I confess to have sinned
grievously, and then had rather not hear music. See now my state: weep
with me, and weep for me, ye, who regulate your feelings within, as that
good action ensues. For you who do not act, these things touch not you. But
Thou, O Lord my God, hearken; behold, and see, and have mercy and heal
me, Thou, in whose presence I have become a problem to myself; and that is
my infirmity.* (Confessions 10:33)

Augustine laments his inner struggle, wishing for less attractive music
so that the words might be given primacy, while acknowledging that the
beauty of the music actually helps to draw some people (perhaps including
himself) to the text. In our study we will continue to observe and explore
how this juncture of intellect and emotion brings conflict within individuals, between individuals, and between religious groups.

The Medieval Period

Church leaders over time established a prescribed order of religious events
and content. By the time of Pope Gregory I (r. 590-604) the preeminence
of the Roman Bishop was generally acknowledged, and within a few centuries the entire Western church was following the liturgy of Rome. Two
broad divisions of the liturgy[7] included the Mass, the daily observance
of the Lord's Supper (or "Eucharist"), along with designated readings,
prayers, and songs; and the Divine Office, celebrated mostly in monasteries, consisting of the eight daily prayers hours.

During this time there was singing by monks in monasteries, by highly
trained and prized musicians in cathedrals, and by nuns in convents.
Congregations were mostly silent, although various local practices were

---

[7] The word "liturgy" derives from the Greek leiturgia, referring to public duties and service. We use the term to refer to the content and order of religious ceremonies.

followed throughout the middle ages regarding congregational participation. In Gregory the Great's time the congregation might participate in reciting:

•the *Kyrie,*

   Lord, have mercy; Christ, have mercy, Lord have mercy

•the *Gloria,*

•and the *Sanctus*

   Holy, holy, holy, Lord God Almighty, Heaven and earth are full of thy glory;

     Hosanna in the highest.

   Blessed is he who comes in the name of the Lord;

     Hosanna in the highest.

With the expansion of the Mass in the seventh century, congregations might join in saying or singing:

•the *Credo* (a slightly altered Nicene Creed),

•and the *Agnus Dei*:

   Lamb of God, who takes away the sins of the world,

     Have mercy on us.

   Lamb of God, who takes away the sins of the world,

     Have mercy on us.

   Lamb of God, who takes away the sins of the world,

     Grant us thy peace.

Although the other songs, readings, and prayers of the Mass changed from week to week, these five portions were almost always present, and they collectively have come to be known as the Ordinary of the Mass.

In the last centuries of the first millennium the privilege of participation was disappearing, and congregations would be largely silent in the church for six hundred years. Eventually, they would again be invited to sing and recite, and much later, when the Second Vatican Council (1962-65) allowed Masses to be celebrated in the vernacular, the texts of the Ordinary have again become ingrained in all Catholic parishioners.

Carolingian influence

By the end of the eighth century, Charlemagne, the King of the Franks, had conquered nearly all of Europe (excluding modern Poland, Spain, and Great Britain). Pope Leo III judiciously offered to acknowledge Charlemagne as the modern successor to Constantine and crowned him "Emperor of the Romans" on Christmas day in 800. In return, Charlemagne solidified the Pope's rule over the Papal States, a large portion of central Italy over which the Pope claimed temporal control.

Charlemagne's reign was an energetic one that emphasized education, the rule of law, trade, economic improvement, and religion. He forced conquered peoples to accept Christianity. And, in order to provide a common heritage and culture, to he infused his polyglot empire with the songs, stories, and traditions of the Roman church.

In this optimistic and fertile environment, clergymen and musicians took Old Roman Chant as the raw material for experimentation and development, and what we call Gregorian chant owes more to the years after Charlemagne's time than to those before. These musicians expanded existing chants and developed new ones; they combined chant with drama, at first in the Christmas and Easter Masses, but later more extravagantly in liturgical drama and mystery plays; they added instruments to supplement the voices; and they investigated and developed polyphony, adding one, two, or even three simultaneous melodies to existing chants. A bishop's status was reflected by the quality of his cathedral choir, and cathedrals and monasteries were fruitful fields for the development of new musical ideas.

In addition to musical developments, the medieval period produced a significant amount of devotional religious poetry which would be translated, adapted, and published in hymnals centuries later. Some bishops, such as Venantius Fortunatus (c.530-609) and Theodulph of Orleans (c.760-821) contributed to this genre. Among the monks and priests whose devotional poems are still sung are Columba (521-97), the Irish missionary to the Scots; Peter Abelard (1079-1142); Bernard of Clairvaux (c.1091-1153, considered by many to be the most likely root source for "Jesus, the Very Thought of Thee," PftL 373; "Jesus, Thou Joy of Loving Hearts," PftL 374; and "O Sacred Head, Now Wounded," PftL 484), Bernard of Cluny (12th century, see PftL 81); and Francis of Assisi (1182-1226; PftL 16 is taken from his "Canticle to the Sun," one of the earliest Italian poems). In the East, Synesius of Cyrene (c.365-c.414), John of Damascus (c.700-c.780), and his nephew Stephen the Sabaite (725-95) wrote Greek poetry that has also been adapted for performance in Western churches.

By the ninth century the Christian church had become irrevocably divided, even though the break was not to be finalized until 1054. In the west, the

Bishop of Rome (by Gregory's time called the Pope) exercised spiritual leadership in a region of shifting secular authorities. The eastern church, centered in Constantinople, operated in a theocracy in which the Emperor and the Patriarch shared power. The two churches followed separate tracks politically and liturgically.

CHAPTER 4

REFORMATION HYMNODY

D uring the fifteenth and sixteenth centuries a tidal shift occurred as the authority, the practices, and the dogma of the medieval church were challenged by an assortment of religious reformers and their followers, and the congregation was again invited to actively participate in meetings. Led by free thinkers in England, Bohemia, Holland, Saxony, France, and Switzerland, revolutionary groups broke from Rome, largely to reconfirm the rights of individuals to have access to God's word and grace without Papal control.

Jan Hus

Jan Hus (1369-1415), a priest in Prague, admired the teachings of the Englishman John Wycliffe (c.1328-84), who had questioned the motives and authority of church leaders and had produced an English translation of the Bible. Because of his attacks on the authority of the church and on the sale of indulgences, Hus was excommunicated in 1412. The Council of Constance in 1415 assured him safety if would come to defend his teachings; nevertheless, upon hearing him present his doctrines the Council found him guilty of heresy and delivered him to the secular authorities to be burned at the stake. He left behind a flock that was sometimes divided, generally persecuted, but often highly committed. And they sang. Hus himself had written some hymns for his congregation,[1] others were added to this collection, and in 1501 Bishop Lucas of Prague published a hymnal containing eighty-nine hymns in Czech. Polish and German versions of their hymns appeared by mid-century. These Bohemian Brethren called themselves the *Unitas Fratrum* (Unity of Brethren), and they pursued disciplined lives, simplicity in worship, a belief in the supreme authority of the Bible, and a regular sharing in the Lord's Supper, of which members

---

[1] It was reported that he sang a hymn as he died at the stake.

were allowed to take the cup as well as the bread. Many of their songs referred to the Lord's Supper; others were songs of encouragement in the face of persecution or calls for steadfastness in armed conflict. Some Hussite hymns were adopted by other German-speaking denominations and spread beyond the group's boundaries. Void of political protection, the Brethren splintered and found refuge in various parts of Europe, including Moravia. This was a small but important movement, one whose story we will encounter again.

The Hussite, Lutheran, and Anabaptist groups mentioned in this chapter brought a different content and function to congregational singing. For them, singing was not solely a means for instruction or an avenue of praise. Their songs, often specific to their own experiences and theology, provided consolation and encouragement in times of struggle,and offered a sense of identity in a continent that was experiencing increasing religious division.

Martin Luther

With Martin Luther (1483-1546) the Reformation hit its full stride. Luther had been trained as a priest in the Catholic Church and by 1512 was a professor of Biblical theology at Wittenberg University. In 1515 the Medicean Pope Leo X authorized Albrecht the Archbishop of Mainz to sell indulgences, largely to provide funds for building the new St. Peter's Cathedral in Rome. Albrecht's indulgence salesman, Johann Tetzel, promised delivery from a certain number of years in Purgatory for one's self or one's relatives, depending upon the payment that was made: "When a coin in the coffer clings, a soul from Purgatory springs!"

This blatant commercialization of grace aroused Luther's anger. He was offended that the Pope required a payment from peasants, who had nothing to spare, when he supposedly could have granted the benefit at no cost. And he was increasingly convinced that the church, in fact, did not control grace. Grace was God's free gift to man, not to be purchased by monetary payment or payment in kind.

Luther wrote a letter of complaint to Albrecht and included a list of ninety-five points of contention. According to tradition, he also posted these ninety-five theses on the church door in Wittenberg on October 31, 1517. Had all of this happened seventy years earlier, Luther would have probably met the same fate as Hus. But by 1517 the printing press had decisively changed the manner of disseminating interesting and controversial information, and Luther's theses were soon in every church, tavern, and council room in Saxony.

Succeeding meetings and publications intensified his conflict with Rome and with the Holy Roman Empire. He was commanded to recant. He did not. In 1521 he was excommunicated by the Pope and declared an outlaw by Emperor Charles V, a declaration which would have shortened his life expectancy considerably had he not been taken into benevolent captivity by Frederick the Wise, the Elector of Saxony.[2] During this year of protective custody he worked on translating the New Testament into German, being convinced that every man should have access to the scriptures.

The reform continued without Luther's personal oversight. Some of his colleagues advocated for even more radical changes, and there were violent acts involving church property and church leaders. Leaving Wartburg in 1522, Luther was able to instill some coherence into the movement.

Luther's arguments with the church were serious, but not comprehensive; he was content with many of its practices and traditions, and his first liturgy retained much of the Latin text and form. The choir played a dominant role, the congregation joining on a few hymns. This was the form he proposed for cathedrals and abbeys where the services were solemn and formal and many participants understood Latin.

But Latin was not a language for commoners, so he produced in 1526 a German Mass, adding congregational hymns. He did not suggest either of

---

[2] Frederick's protection of Luther was a matter of conscience and not economy. Granted, he and other German princes were glad to consider the possibility of escaping their obligation to Rome. But Frederick owned a collection of relics that could grant anyone who observed them, accompanied by the payment of the proper indulgences, a reduction of one's stay in Purgatory by 1,902,202 years and 270 days. This was a source of comfort to him and of income to his treasury that would lose much of its financial worth as the spiritual value of relics and indulgences was refuted.

these liturgies as a required or invariable form; congregations were free to alter them and to use Latin and/or German as circumstances required.

Spiritual songs in the vernacular had ample precedent in German lands. *Leisen*[3] and other sacred songs were already established in the traditions of the people and were used in schools, in homes, on pilgrimages, and in churches; and much of the repertoire of the *Minnesingers* and *Meistersingers* was on sacred texts. Some hymns from the Hussite Bohemian Brethren were adopted by Luther's associates. It was with Luther and his followers that vernacular hymnody became common in German-speaking territories and widely exposed to the rest of the world.

Luther's first collection of chorales, commonly called the *Achtliederbuch*, was published in 1524. For these eight songs he himself contributed four texts and two tunes; he was a talented amateur musician and an experienced writer. The publication also included theological commentary on the texts, because there were those who were still suspicious of hymns not taken directly from scripture.

In a number of chorales the first portion of the tune is repeated, following the pattern of the "bar form" (AAB) that was common in German songs of this period. It was also fairly common to recall the "A" section at the end of the song, and many of the tunes conclude with a descending scale. Chorales were intended for unison congregational singing, and Luther apparently preferred no instrumental accompaniment, though he used an organ to set the key.

The psalm settings represent Luther's desire to maintain the Psalter's place in the liturgy. In addition to Psalms 46 and 130 Luther also versified Psalms 12 (*Ach Gott von Himmel sieh darein*) and 67 (*Es wollt uns Gott gnädig sein*). As would Watts nearly 200 years later, he adapted the psalms' texts to fit current circumstances.

One of these songs for which he was both author and composer was *Aus tiefer Not*, an adaptation of Psalm 130. Luther gave the Psalm a Christian flavor, emphasizing God's grace and mercy. This was to be one of his and his followers' favorite hymns; it was sung by the crowds lining the streets

---

[3] *Leisen* were folk hymns in German, sung at festivals and on pilgrimages, which often ended with the words "Kyrie eleison"; hence the term "Leisen."

of Halle in 1546 as his coffin was carried toward Wittenberg, his burial place.

Aus tiefer Not

Aus tie-fer Not schrei ich zu dir, Herr Gott, er-hör mein Ru - fen;
Dein gnä-dig Ohr neig her zu mir Und mei-ner Bitt sie öff - ne!

Denn so du willt das se - hen an, Was Sünd und Un-recht

ist__ ge - tan, Wer kann, Herr, vor dir blei - ben?

Out of the depths I cry to you; O Father, hear me calling.
Incline your ear to my distress In spite of my rebelling.
Do not regard my sinful deeds. Send me the grace my spirit needs;
Without it I am nothing.

All things you send are full of grace; You crown our lives with favor.
All our good works are done in vain Without our Lord and Savior.
We praise the God who gives us faith And saves us from the grip of death;
Our lives are in his keeping.

It is in God that we shall hope, And not in our own merit.
We rest our fears in his good Word And trust his Holy Spirit.
His promise keeps us strong and sure; We trust the holy signature
Inscribed upon our temples.

My soul is waiting for the Lord As one who longs for morning,
No watcher waits with greater hope Than I for his returning.
I hope as Israel in the Lord; He sends redemption through his Word.
We praise him for his mercy.

Another early collection for the congregation, to be used at home and in church, was the *Erfurt Enchiridion* (1524), with twenty-six texts and sixteen melodies. Luther was to eventually write about three dozen texts and a few tunes. His best-known composition is *Ein feste Burg*, based on Psalm 46, which first appeared in 1529.

Ein feste Burg

Ein' fes - te Burg ist un - ser Gott, Ein' gu - te wehr und waf - fen.
Er hilft uns frei aus al - ler Not die uns jetzt hat be- trof - fen.

Der alt'___ bö - se Feind mit Ernst er's jetzt meint; Gross' Macht und viel'

List sei' graus - am' Rus - tung ist; auf Erd'n ist nicht sein's Glei - chen.

A mighty fortress is our God, A sword and shield victorious;
He breaks the cruel oppressor's rod And wins salvation glorious.
The old evil foe, Sworn to work us woe,
With dread craft and might He arms himself to fight.
On Earth he has no equal.

No strength of ours can match his might! We would be lost, rejected.
But now a champion comes to fight, Whom God himself elected.
Ask who this may be: Lord of Hosts is he!
Jesus Christ our Lord, God's only son, adored.
He holds the field victorious.

Though hordes of devils fill the land All threat'ning to devour us,
We tremble not, unmoved we stand; They cannot overpow'r us.
This world's prince may rage, In fierce war engage.
He is doomed to fail; God's judgement must prevail!
One little word subdues him.

God's word forever shall abide, No thanks to foes, who fear it;
For God himself fights by our side With weapons of the Spirit.
If they take our house, Goods, fame, child or spouse,
Wrench our life away, They cannot win the day.
The Kingdom's ours forever!

The tunes were sturdy and evocative, often with a rugged rhythm that did not survive later arrangements.[4] An accomplished singer and instrumentalist, Luther judged that the message of the tune must be paired carefully with the message of the text. When he was preparing the *Deutscher Messe* he enlisted the aid of Johann Walter, the Kapellmeister to the Elector of Saxony, and he was determined that every note of the music would contribute to the total effect of the message. Said Walter, "He kept me three weeks long at Wittenberg, to write out the notes over some of the Gospels and Epistles, until the first German Mass was sung in the parish church."[5]

Luther considered music to be the servant of the text, providing the perfect setting in which the meaning and sense of the hymn could be seen most clearly, and it was prepared by an artisan rather than by an artist. "Whether you wish to comfort the sad, to subdue frivolity, to encourage the despairing, to humble the proud, to calm the passionate, or to appease those full of hate . . . what more effective means than music could you find?"[6]

Some of the tunes that Luther used were adapted from plainsong or from German secular songs.[7] He used the tune of *Wach auf, wach auf, du schöne* ("Wake up, wake up, you beauty") for *Nun freut euch, lieben Christen g'mein* ("Dear Christians, one and all, rejoice"). Some hymns of the Hussite Bohemian Brethren were used by Luther's followers.

In other cases, however, the secular association was too strong to overcome; for example, he adapted the tune *Aus fremden Landen komm' ich her* for his song *Vom Himmel hoch da komm ich her*. When he realized that the tune maintained an unbreakable connection with taverns and dance halls, he felt compelled to devise a different tune for his chorale.

Succeeding generations of evangelical musicians would follow Luther's lead, occasionally pairing hymn texts with appropriate secular tunes to

---

[4] It is interesting to compare the free and robust rhythms of Luther's *Ein feste Burg* tune with the familiar arrangement and harmonization by J. S. Bach, which is much more foursquare and musically proper.

[5] Piero Weiss and Richard Taruskin, *Music in the Western World* (New York: Schirmer Books, 1984), 104.

[6] Martin Luther, quoted in Wilson-Dickson, *The Story of Christian Music*, p. 60

[7] According to *The Monthly Review, or, Literary Journal*, Vol. 49 (June 1773 - January 1774), p. 430, George Whitefield was later to ask, "Why should the devil have all the best tunes?"

produce works which came to be known as *contrafacta* (singular, *con-trafactum* — "counterfeit"); as when Hassler's tune *Mein Gmüth ist mir verwirret* ("I'm all confused by the charms of a tender maid") was used for a text translated from Latin, *O Haupt voll Blut und Wunden* ("O Sacred Head, Now Wounded," PftL 484); and Isaac's *Innsbruck, ich muss dich lassen* ("Innsbruck, I Now Must Leave You") became *O Welt, ich muss dich lassen* ("O world I now must leave you") and, later, *Nun ruhen alle Wälder* ("Now Rest Beneath Night's Shadow," PftL 455).

Though early chorales were published with tunes only, without harmony, Luther worked with Johann Walter to publish the *Wittenberg Gesangbuch* in 1524, in which chorales were arranged for four voices. The intent was, as Luther explained in the preface, to appeal to young people, who were musically educated and involved. Walter later published his own *Gesang-büchlein*, with the polyphonic settings in two styles: one following the older tradition of placing the melody in the tenor part, with decorative lines in the other voices; the other in the newer "cantional" style, placing the tune in the top voice while the other voices sang simple note-against-note harmony (as was to become common in later congregational singing).

Luther's own textual and musical contributions were not insignificant. However, his greatest contribution to congregational singing was his insistence that it should, in fact, exist. Many of his followers, at his urging, tried their hands at poetry and tune-smithing, and by the end of the century there were over 1500 publications of German chorales. Their aim was set high, considering their high opinion of their mentor's output. Cyriacus Spangenburg, in the year before Luther's death, wrote in a preface to a 1545 publication of his sermons on Luther's hymns:

> One must certainly let this be true, and remain true, that among all Mas-tersingers from the days of the Apostles until now, Luther is and always will be the best and most accomplished; in whose hymns and songs one does not find a vain or needless word. All flows and falls in the sweetest and neat-est manner, full of spirit and doctrine, so that his every word gives outright a sermon of his own, or at least a singular reminiscence. There is nothing forced, nothing foisted in or patched up, nothing fragmentary. The rhymes are easy and good, the words choice and proper, the meaning clear and in-telligible, the melodies lovely and hearty, and — in summa — all is so rare and majestic, so full of pith and power, so cheering and comforting, that, in sooth, you will not find his equal, much less his master.[8]

---

[8] quoted in *The Christian Examiner*, 1860

German congregational singing after Luther

Among the sixteenth-century publications of German church music, some were psalters, some contained a mixture of Latin and German texts, some contained new works, and others were large collections of the most popular chorales. Some contained settings of such complexity that they were obviously intended for the choir or the organ. Others were in simple four-part settings. In 1586 Lukas Osiander published *Fünfzig geistliche Lieder und Psalmen* in cantional style; Hans Leo Hassler's *Kirchengesänge, Psalmen und geistliche Lieder* of 1608 proved that congregational singing was alive in the first part of the new century.

The phenomenon of German congregational singing, however, proved to be more exportable than entrenched. The German evangelical church never lost its love for the choir and for sophisticated music. In smaller churches, it is true, congregational participation continued; however, in larger churches that could afford strong musical establishments, it declined. At the beginning of the seventeenth century many congregations sang chorales, but as the century progressed more and more of the stanzas were sung by the choir or played by the organist. In J.S. Bach's eighteenth-century Leipzig the congregation listened more than it sang, perhaps joining the orchestra and chorus only occasionally for a stanza of a chorale. By 1800 many chorale books contained only words, without tunes, and contemporaneous accounts sometimes described Lutheran congregational singing as being dismal, especially noting slow tempos, with each note of a chorale requiring from two to four seconds. Those who supported this performance mode said that a faster pace was undignified.

A collection consisting mostly of Latin hymns compiled by a Lutheran pastor and published by a Catholic Finnish student, was printed in 1582 in Sweden. The songs in *Piae Cantiones* were popular in Finland and Sweden; a Finnish version appeared in 1616. Some of the tunes entered the English repertoire after a copy of the first edition was given in 1853 to John Mason Neale, who wrote the poem "Good King Wenceslas" to go with the tune TEMPUS ADEST FLORIDUM. Other tunes from the collection include PERSONENT HODIE and RESONET IN LAUDIBUS.

One of the most enduring of the German tunes appeared in 1623 in a Catholic publication from Cologne. We show it here in its original version, but by 1625 it had been adopted by other religious groups, copied, and revised into the tune that now appears in many hymnals (found in a later harmonization by Ralph Vaughan Williams at PftL 16).

Lasst uns erfreuen

Lasst uns er-freu-en herz-lich sehr. Al-le-lu-ia!
Ma-ri-a seufzt und weint nicht mehr. Al-le-lu-ia!

Ver-schwun-den al-le Ü-bel sein, Al-le-lu-ia!
Jetzt glänzt der hel-le Son-nen-schein. Al-le-lu-ia!

Al-le-lu-ia! Al-le-lu-ia! Al-le-lu-ia!

Let us rejoice heartily.
Mary sighs and cries no more.
All evils have disappeared
Now the bright sunshine shines.

Pietism

In 1644 Johann Crüger, influenced by French psalters that had been brought to Berlin by Calvinists, published his *Praxis Pietatis Melica*. The collection included "Nun danket alle Gott" (PftL 457 and 458) and "Jesu meine Freude" (PftL 361), both of which are widely sung. But the course of hymnody was already being reshaped by circumstances that dramatically changed the lives and attitudes of many German-speaking people.

The Thirty Years' War (1618-48) was devastating to Germans. Approximately a fifth of them lost their lives during the conflict, and it took years for agriculture and commerce to recover. As an example of the war's atrocities, consider the actions of General Albrecht von Wallenstein, who was given permission by the Emperor to allow his troops to pillage freely in both enemy and friendly territories. His army of over 50,000 warriors brought indiscriminate destruction to much of central Europe and contributed to a growing skepticism regarding church and political institutions in the minds of many.

Partially as a result of this distrust, a religious movement arising in the second half of the century emphasized personal, rather than institutional, devotion to God. Pietism, as the movement was called, was also influenced by the personal sufferings experienced by many during the war and by the cumulative effects of previous and ongoing Restoration movements.

The leader of the movement, Philip Jakob Spener (1635-1705) of Strasbourg (later of Frankfurt and Berlin), actually defined his goal as a second, more complete Restoration, honoring Luther while recognizing his inadequacies. According to Spener and his followers, experience is the basis for knowledge. Consequently, religious experience trumps dogma: only a regenerated Christian can be trusted to truly understand Christian doctrine.

Pietists tended to believe that traditional liturgy and symbolism had lost their significance; they often turned from conventional religious meetings to house churches and from traditional chorales to more intimate songs, often solos accompanied by organs, expressing personal faith and commitment. Texts sometimes emphasized painful details of Christ's suffering. The tunes of the Pietists tended to be less sturdy and more emotional and folkish than those of the traditional church.

One of the more magnetic figures among the Pietists was Joachim Neander (1650-80), a German Calvinist, who was, in turn, an undisciplined student, a reformed Christian, a schoolteacher, and a meditative hermit. For the last part of his life, he lived in a cave, where he wrote poetry and tunes, including those we know as "Praise to the Lord, the Almighty" (PftL 534) and ARNSBERG (PftL 177).

Perhaps the most mystical of the Pietist poets was Gerhard Tersteegen (author of "God Himself is With Us," PftL 177). The fifth stanza of his "Thou Hidden Love of God" was translated thus by John Wesley:

Each moment draw from earth away
  My heart that lowly waits thy call;
Speak to my inmost soul and say,
  "I am thy Love, thy god, thy all!"
To feel thy power, to hear thy voice,
To taste thy love, be all my choice.

The Lutheran church was especially impacted by the movement and for fifty years was divided into Orthodox and Pietist camps, with Pietists eschewing traditional chorales in favor of more personal and sentimental expression. A gradual reconciliation came about during the early eighteenth century when Orthodox centers began to include devotional poetry in their services, often coupled with traditional chorales. Many of Bach's cantatas illustrate this type of pairing.

Erdmann Neumeister, a pastor in Hamburg (and a friend of Bach), wrote some of these devotional verses, though he was not allied with the Pietist movement. One of his poems, "Jesus nimmt die Sünder an," is today known in its translation by Emma Bevan (see PftL 588); here are its four stanzas, set to the tune VOLLER WUNDER, by J. G. Ebeling (1637-76).

Sinners Jesus Will Receive

Erdmann Neumeister, trans. Emma Bevan   VOLLER WUNDER

Shepherds seek their wandering sheep
o'er the mountains bleak and cold;
Jesus such a watch doth keep
o'er the lost ones of his fold,
seeking them o'er moor and fen:
Christ receiveth sinful men.

Sick and sorrowful and blind,
I with all my sins draw nigh;
O my Savior, thou canst find
help for sinners such as I;
speak that word of love again,
"Christ receiveth sinful men."

Christ receiveth sinful men,
even me, with all my sin;
openeth to me heaven again;
with him I may enter in.
Death hath no more sting nor pain;
Christ receiveth sinful men.

Chorales continued to be written and published, but they never again engaged congregations as they had in the early years of the Reformation.

Zwingli and the Anabaptists

Ulrich Zwingli (1484-1531) of Zürich was ordained as a Catholic priest in 1506, but the influences of Erasmus and Luther led him to a reformed theology. Following his influence, the city voted in 1523 to break from the Roman church.[9] Zwingli was a pragmatic, rational leader who organized services that were more didactic than colorful, omitting music altogether because of its potential for seduction of the senses, and preferring responsive recitation of psalms and canticles.

A number of Zwingli's followers, encouraged to value scriptural teaching more highly than church doctrine or tradition, came to believe that baptism

---

[9] The concept of individual freedom of religion is relatively recent. Throughout most of history, rulers were expected to establish the religious climate, and citizens to comply.

was a matter for adult believers rather than infants. Zwingli found adult baptism an impractical proposal and refused to support them. Dissatisfied, the "Anabaptists" ("re-baptists") broke away and established religious communities. They came to be known as the Brethren and were persecuted equally by Catholics and Protestants, to the point of death. Faced with constant danger, they turned to song for comfort and encouragement. Their first songbook was published in 1564, with many of its texts written by believers who had been arrested for their doctrine; it was entitled *Etliche schöne christliche Gesäng wie dieselbigen zu Passau von den Schweizer Brüdern in der Gefenknus im Schloss durch göttliche Gnade gedicht und gesungen warden* ("Genuinely Beautiful Christian Songs Which Were Written and Sung Through God's Grace by the Swiss Brethren in the Passau Castle Prison") and commonly called the *Ausbund*. Its texts were largely a celebration of the triumph of God's people in a fallen, sorrowful, lonely world. The songs would be sung to familiar tunes; the collection contained no printed notes.

The Brethren were scattered throughout Germany, Switzerland, Holland, and Bohemia, proclaiming in song and teaching that God's true followers, in whatever place or time, would suffer persecution and martyrdom. Their songs were in the vernacular and sung without instruments. Some were imported from Holland or north Germany or borrowed from the Bohemian Brethren. The songbook was reissued in a number of expanded versions, never including musical notation but often with a notice indicating the name of the tune to be used. These were often well-known popular or folk tunes, and the pairing of text and tune sometimes made a strange match — as when a song describing the martyrdom of a brother was assigned the tune "There Was a Maiden with a Jug." As late as 1692 the *Ausbund* was on the proscribed list of publications in Bern, Switzerland.

Many of the Brethren came to be called Mennonites, after Menno Simons (ca. 1496-1561), an influential leader in Holland and Germany. In the 1690s Jacob Ammann led a dissenting group, to be called the Amish, which favored a stricter church discipline regarding those who had left the fellowship. The Old Amish Order in this country still uses an edition of the *Ausbund*, which thus becomes the oldest hymnal in continuous use any-where, and their most representative song, the *Loblied*[10] ("Praise song"), is sung regularly at church meetings and weddings. The Old Amish and

---

[10] See "A hymn of the Old Order" by Myron K. Sauder, *The Hymn*, Vol. 62, No. 2, pp. 58-61 for background on this hymn.

some Mennonites still sing in German; observers of this traditional singing remark that it is notable for the slowness of tempo.[11]

Here is an English translation of a song from the *Ausbund*.[12]

> *Look at Christ the friendly knight! Look at the captain! The battle, when you come to this place, is fierce. The enemies — the world, the flesh, sin, the devil, and death — close in around you. But leap to your captain's side! He will kill the enemies! He will help you out of all distress. Stay with your flag! Do not let them drive you back from your captain, Jesus Christ! If you want the crown and the glory, and if you want to triumph with him, you must suffer and die with him too. They caught Christ our captain and beat him. In like manner they mistreat us, his followers. The hour of distress has come upon all the earth. They hunt us out. In almost every country they try to catch us because we stand for Christ. They try to keep Christ from coming to help us, barricading all the roads until they have us. Then the strangling and the stabbing, the gruesome violence begins. But wait, our captain, he will avenge it! He will break the power of the enemy, and he will stand with his little flock!*
>
> *All you beloved knights of God, be strong! Be manly in the fight! This dreadful storm will not be long. Stand fast! Stand true to death! Do not allow them to drive you back. Men and women, trust in God!*

Most Christians today would find the long hymns awkward and cumbersome for worship assemblies and social gatherings, but they were pertinent and powerful to the early Brethren. This songbook, with its emphasis on fortitude in the face of persecution, its lists and accounts of martyrs, and its comparison of Christ's suffering with ours was not a mere hymnbook. It provided historical accounts, a collection of folklore, a church's patriotic songs, a repertoire of rallying cries. More than any collection of Christian texts that had been written until that time, it recalled the centrality of communal identity found in the Jewish psalms and canticles.

The Anabaptists were not the only group to face persecution. Other fellowships endured their own struggles and produced their own songs of

---

[11] There are reports from many different traditions about the slowness of congregational singing. Edmund Gosse (1849-1928) wrote in *Father and Son* (New York: Charles Scribner's Sons, 1907, p. 91) of his father's participation in meetings with the Plymouth Brethren in London: "He had at least great fondness for singing hymns, in the manner then popular with the Evangelicals, very loudly, and so slowly that I used to count how many words I could read silently, between one syllable of the singing and another."

[12] *Ausbund* 78, as translated by Peter Hoover, quoted from his book *The Secret of Their Strength*, published by Benchmark Press, 1593 Pinola Road, Shippensburg, PA 17257

encouragement. The familiar "We Gather Together," originally published by Adrianus Valerius in his 1626 *Nederlandtsche Gedenckclanck*, speaks for Dutch Protestants who were seeking political and religious independence from the Holy Roman Empire (PftL 705).

We gather together to ask the Lord's blessing,
He chastens and hastens His will to make known;
The wicked oppressing now cease from distressing,
Sing praises to His name - He forgets not His own.

Beside us to guide us, our God with us joining,
Ordaining, maintaining His kingdom divine,
So from the beginning the fight we were winning;
Thou, Lord, wast at our side, all glory be Thine.

We all do extol Thee, Thou Leader triumphant,
And pray that Thou still our defender wilt be.
Let Thy congregation escape tribulation!
Thy name be ever praised! O Lord, make us free!

The expanding reach of song

We have noted that songs preserved from the early centuries of the church were often hymns, praising the Godhead. When reformers such as Hus, Luther, and the Anabaptist groups reestablished congregational singing in the fifteenth and sixteenth centuries, their adherents still sang praises — but they also sang about their existential circumstances, exhorting each other to maintain faith in the face of persecution, to recognize the nature of the spiritual battle in which they were engaged, to look to the ultimate triumph in the next life, and to support each other through fellowship and encouragement. Hymns often imparted a sense of religious identity and brotherhood.

The songs of the Pietist movement were also purposeful, with the goal of identifying and establishing intimate relationships between believers and the Lord. While they recall the spirit of much of the medieval devotional poetry produced in cathedrals and monasteries, their audience was expanded, taking the expression of personal communion with God from the cells of the monasteries to the hearts of all who were willing.

CHAPTER 5

Reformation Psalmody

Hus, Luther, and the Anabaptists composed and sang hymns. Others believed that God had already provided all of the words needed to praise him, without the need for texts "of human composure."[1] The primary leaders in this tradition were Jean Calvin in Geneva and Henry VIII and Thomas Cranmer in England.

Jean Calvin

Jean Calvin (1509-64), a Frenchman who had studied at the University of Paris, declared himself a Protestant in 1533 and moved to Switzerland, where he published the first edition of his *Institutes of the Christian Religion*. This work brought immediate attention, and he was called to Geneva, which had just broken with the Catholic Church. His attempts to establish a Protestant theocracy there met with resistance, and he was asked to leave the city.

He moved to Strasbourg and pastored a group of French Protestant refugees. There he was introduced to the singing of metrical psalms, particularly those of Clement Marot, a favorite poet at the court of King Francis I of France, where Marot had introduced versified psalms. In Geneva, music had not been allowed. Having experienced the Strasbourg assembly, Calvin came to the pragmatic conclusion that singing was the most effective way for a congregation to learn and recite psalms, and he determined to produce a complete versified psalter. He took a dozen of Marot's psalm settings, added six of his own, and published a partial psalter in 1539.

---

[1] II Peter 1:3: "His divine power has given us everything we need for a godly life …."

After a change of government in Geneva, Calvin was invited in 1541 to return to a leadership role in the church and the city. One of his first moves was to establish the congregational singing of a psalm each Sunday before the sermon. Later this plan was amended to include more congregational singing, so that eventually the congregation sang the entire psalter twice during each year.[2] There was no serious consideration of hymnody, since Calvin and his associates believed that God should be praised only with His own words. Calvin acknowledged that hymns were sung by early Christians but asserted that these were conveyed as a gift of the Spirit. In addition to psalms, Calvin allowed congregational musical presentation of the Ten Commandments, the *Nunc dimittis*, and the Apostles' Creed.[3]

An ally soon appeared to assist Calvin in his task. In 1542 Marot published a volume of thirty psalm versifications, which, unfortunately for him, was happily taken up by the Huguenots, French Protestants. As he became associated with Protestantism in the public's opinion, Marot was forced to leave France. He chose Geneva for his sanctuary, and he continued his writing so that he had completed forty-nine of the psalms by the time of his death in 1544.

After Marot's death, Calvin recruited another writer and scholar, Theodore Beza, to finish the work, and the complete *Genevan Psalter* was published in 1562. Most of the tunes for the collection were produced by the French musician Louis Bourgeois.[4] And "tunes" is the correct term, for Calvin allowed only unison, unaccompanied singing, believing that this mode of presentation would be appropriately simple, majestic, and indicative of the unity of the believers. He was suspicious of the four- and five-part musical settings which soon appeared among his followers for home use; and,

---

[2] Heather Josselyn-Cranson, "Gaining a New Appreciation for Calvin and Music," *The Hymn*, Vol.63, No. 3, Summer 2012, p. 24.

[3] The Apostles' Creed, or *Symbolum Apostolorum*, is a statement of faith of ancient, though indeterminate, origin.

[4] Bourgeois was a colorful and influential musician, who gained some notoriety in his reformation of the five-century-old method of sight-singing which had been developed by Guido of Arezzo. He spent a night in prison in 1551 in Geneva for altering psalm tunes without authorization, causing confusion among some parishioners who had learned the previous tunes by heart; he was released with Calvin's personal intervention and soon left Geneva. He differed with Calvin's opinion that congregational singing should be unaccompanied, claiming that some of the psalms practically required instrumental participation. He was a musician more than a reformer; his daughter was later baptized into the Catholic Church in Paris.

according to some accounts, he and Bourgeois fell out over the latter's attempts to introduce four-part singing into the churches.

The tunes were syllabic and simple, with generally only two note values (short and long), and the melodies moved mostly by steps and small intervals. Some were newly composed and some were taken from other sources: the melody for Psalm 129 was taken directly from the morning hymn for the feast of St. Benedict. Despite Calvin's austerity (he removed sculptures and ornamentation from the churches and wore a plain black gown when he preached), many of the tunes had such a distinctive rhythmic lilt that detractors such as Elizabeth I, comparing them to the simplicity of plainsong, derisively called them "Genevan jigs." Here is the first stanza of Psalm 42, by Bourgeois and Beza, with an English translation from the Psalter Hymnal published in 1987 by the Christian Reformed Church (Goudimel's harmonization of this tune is at PftL 109 with different words).

Genevan Psalm 42

Here is Psalm 124, again with an English translation of the text. We print it here in the impossible key in which it appeared in the Genevan publication, reminding us that transposition (raising or lowering the pitch of the song) was expected.

Genevan Psalm 124

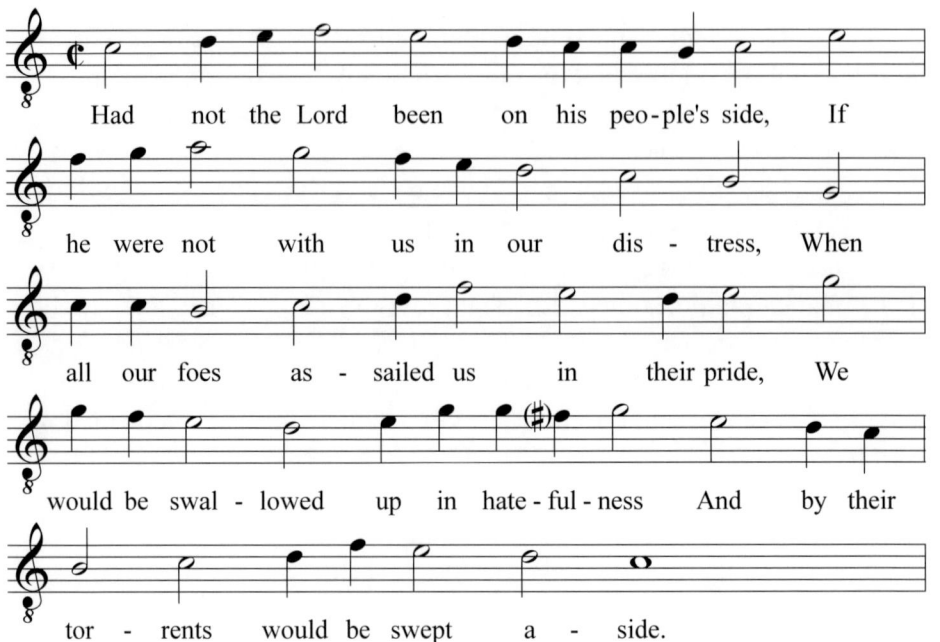

Had not the Lord been on his peo-ple's side, If
he were not with us in our dis - tress, When
all our foes as - sailed us in their pride, We
would be swal - lowed up in hate - ful - ness And by their
tor - rents would be swept a - side.

The 1562 publication included 150 psalms, with 125 tunes in 110 meters,[5] so most of the psalms were identified with a particular tune. In addition, the collection included the Ten Commandments and the Nunc Dimittis. It was soon translated into more than twenty languages.

The French psalter provided source material for a number of composers who adapted its contents for their own purposes. Bourgeois produced some four-part settings for use outside of the assembly. Claude Goudimel arranged about sixty of the psalms in motet style, intended for accomplished singers rather than congregations, publishing them between 1551 and 1566. In 1564 and 1565, immediately following Calvin's death, he published two collections of four-part settings in a homophonic style. In his preface to the Genevan edition of 1565 he insisted that these settings were to be used at home, not in the assembly, probably because Calvin had insisted on unison singing in the assemblies. Here is Goudimel's arrangement of Psalm 100 from that collection, with William Kethe's English setting of the same Psalm.

---

[5] "Meter," in this case, refers to the pattern and number of syllables contained in the lines of a stanza. For example, the meter for Psalm 42 is 8 7 8 7 7 7 8 8; the meter for Psalm 100 is 8 8 8 8.

Goudimel's Psalm 100

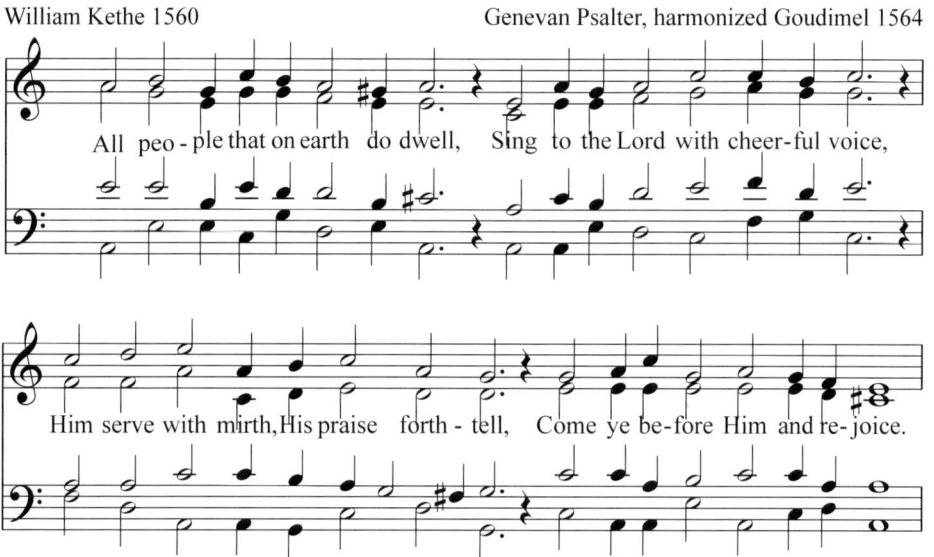

William Kethe 1560   Genevan Psalter, harmonized Goudimel 1564

All peo - ple that on earth do dwell, Sing to the Lord with cheer-ful voice,

Him serve with mirth, His praise forth - tell, Come ye be-fore Him and re-joice.

Henry VIII and the Anglican Church

The leaders of the Reformation did not have religious freedom as their goal. Centuries earlier the Roman government had told its citizens when, where, and how to practice their religion, and the model had not changed (Poland and, later, the Netherlands were the only countries in the sixteenth and seventeenth centuries in which religious persecution was uncommon). The aim of Luther, Zwingli, Calvin, and their collaborators was to free their religious institutions from Roman dogma and control — not to encourage citizens to follow their consciences. Luther, in fact, believed it impractical to consider that different religions could coexist within the

same jurisdiction; civil war was bound to result. Reformers offered greater religious participation to congregants — but not greater freedom.

And if the Reformation on the continent was not about religious freedom, the Reformation in Great Britain was (at least in its beginnings) hardly about religion at all. Henry VIII was married to his older brother's widow, Catherine of Aragon, the daughter of Ferdinand and Isabella of Spain. When, for various reasons, he decided that he did not wish to remain married to Catherine, he asked Pope Clement VII to annul the marriage. This request was made at an inopportune time for the Pope and for Henry, since Rome had just been occupied by the troops of Charles V, the Holy Roman Emperor, who was Catherine's nephew. Even if there had been legitimate reasons for an annulment, the Pope could not and would not cooperate in disgracing the aunt of the Emperor and labeling his cousin Mary an illegitimate child.

Thus England began separating from Rome. Thomas Cranmer, the newly appointed Archbishop of Canterbury, annulled Henry's marriage to Catherine; Henry married Anne Boleyn; and Parliament, in a series of acts, declared that England would not obey any foreign power, that the Church of England was independent of Rome, and that the King was its head.

Henry dissolved the monasteries and claimed their resources, further insulating his country from Catholic tradition (and, not incidentally, acquiring one-quarter of all of the wealth in England). His goal was political and economic, not spiritual reform, and he was not in any way a disciple of Wycliffe, Luther, or Calvin. In 1521 Pope Leo X had responded to Henry's *Defense of the Seven Sacraments*, an attack on Luther's teachings, by naming Henry "Defender of the Faith." When Miles Coverdale published in 1536 a collection of translated Lutheran chorales and other hymns under the title *Goostly Psalms and Spirituall Songes*, Henry put the book on the list of forbidden publications. In the same year, Henry had William Tyndale executed for translating the Bible into English.

Henry died in 1547, and nine-year-old Edward VI succeeded him. During Edward's six-year reign (he died of tuberculosis at the age of fifteen) he and Cranmer carried out a series of religious reforms, designating English as the language of the church, limiting daily services to two (Morning and Evening Prayer), ordaining *The Book of Common Prayer* for use throughout England, and simplifying church music. However, singing was still largely the province of the choir.

Upon Edward's death, his cousin the Lady Jane Grey was placed on the throne. But she ruled only nine days before being deposed (and later beheaded), and Catherine's daughter Mary replaced her. During her five-year reign she actively sought to restore Catholicism in Great Britain. Had she lived longer, she might have been successful. Her marriage to Philip II of

Spain was unpopular, since many considered Spain to be England's great-est enemy. The first woman to rule in her own right as the English Queen, Mary's official title was Mary I, but she is often called "Bloody Mary," since over three hundred people were beheaded or burned at the stake dur-ing her reign. Many of them, including Cranmer, were Protestant leaders. These deaths were chronicled in Foxe's *Book of Martyrs* (1563).

Many Anglicans of influence fled to the continent for safety during her reign, mostly to the Netherlands, Germany, or Switzerland. About 180 households took refuge in Geneva, where nearly one-half of the population consisted of foreign Protestants and Calvin was at his peak as a teacher and administrator (he was to establish the University of Geneva in 1559). Calvin was convincing in discourse and lecture, and many of these "Mar-ian exiles," returning to their homeland after Mary's death, would remain committed to his ideas about election, church governance, and congrega-tional psalmody.

Sternhold and Hopkins

Coincidentally, the Englishmen who fled to Geneva were not unfamiliar with metrical psalmody. Just as Marot had intrigued the French court with his versifications, Thomas Sternhold had taken a similar course in London. Sternhold had been the Groom of the Royal Wardrobe for Henry VIII and later for young Edward VI. He was concerned with the young king's spiri-tual growth and disturbed with the trivial and sometimes bawdy ballads which surrounded him. Cranmer had abolished hymnody, conforming to the wishes of Henry VIII, so Sternhold was unable to write original sacred poems for young Edward's ears. His remedy was to set selected psalms to verse, in the same meter as the court ballads,[6] so that the psalms could be sung to familiar tunes and the young king could be edified by hearing God's words sung. Psalm singing, private and public, was encouraged in the 1549 Act of Uniformity:

> *Provided also that it shal be lawful for al men, as well in churches,*
> *chapels, oratories, or other places, to use openly any Psalm or*
> *Prayer taken out of the bible, at any due time; not letting or omitting*
> *thereby the service, or any part thereof mentioned in the said book.*

---

[6] "Ballade Meter" is 8 6 8 6. That is, there are eight syllables in the first line, six in the second, eight in the third, and six in the fourth. When referring to church tunes, this is called "Common Meter."

Sternhold's first collection of seventeen psalms was published a year or two before his death in 1549. This is his rendering of the first Psalm.

> *1 The man is blest that hath not lent / to wicked men his ear,*
> *Nor led his life as sinners do, / nor sat in scorner's chair.*
> *2 But in the law of God the Lord / doth set his whole delight,*
> *And in the same doth exercise / himself both day and night.*
> *3 He shall be like a tree that is / planted the rivers nigh,*
> *Which in due season bringeth forth / its fruit abundantly;*
> *4 Whose leaf shall never fade nor fall, / but flourishing shall stand:*
> *E'en so all things shall prosper well / that this man takes in hand.*
> *5 As for ungodly men, with them / it shall be nothing so;*
> *But as the chaff, which by the wind / is driven to and fro.*
> *6 Therefore the wicked men shall not / in judgment stand upright,*
> *Nor in th' assembly of the just / shall sinners come in sight.*
> *7 For why? The way of godly men / unto the Lord is known:*
> *Whereas the way of wicked men / shall quite be overthrown.*

A second edition, published after his death, contained eighteen more Sternhold versifications and seven new ones by John Hopkins. The absence of tunes in both publications is another indication that these psalms were written to be sung to the familiar ballad tunes. This collection was brought to Geneva by the refugees, and in 1556 they published an *Anglo-Genevan Psalter* for their own use, with fifty-one psalms, using English and French tunes. They would publish two more editions in Geneva, the last containing eighty-seven psalms.

Mary I died in 1558 and was succeeded by Elizabeth I, the Protestant daughter of Henry and Anne Boleyn, and the religious exiles began returning home. They soon completed the entire Psalter, and in 1562 John Day published *The Whole Book of Psalms*, often referred to as "Sternhold and Hopkins" (later commonly called "The Old Version"), with a title page that, as was customary, included not only the work's title but also its contents, background, and intended function:

The Whole Booke of Psalmes, collected into Englysh metre by T. Starnhold J. Hopkins & others: conferred with the Ebrue, with apt Notes to synge the withal, Faithfully perused and alowed according to thordre appointed in the Quenes maiesties Iniunctions. Very mete to be used of all sortes of people priuately for their solace and comfort: laying apart all ungodly Songes and Ballades, which tende only to the norishing of vyce, and corrupting of youth. . . . Lõdon: John Day, 1562.

Along with the 150 psalms there were versified Biblical texts and a few hymns. The tunes were not harmonized, and there were only forty-seven of them, mostly in Ballad Meter (8.6.8.6), establishing the groundwork for the interchangeability of text and tune that was to become characteristic of English psalmody. Day established another tradition to be followed in later psalters, that of including an introduction to the fundamentals of music.

This publication was a private one, not underwritten by the church. But psalm singing was practiced congregationally in a few churches and became popular in many homes. Day's subsequent publication of a four-part version of the psalter reminds us that the educated English enjoyed hearing and singing harmonies. This harmonized edition appeared in 1563 — twenty-five years before the Italian-inspired *Musica transalpina*, a collection of madrigals that caught the fancy of the next generation of Britons.

The title page of a 1572 edition notes that the psalms could be sung
> *before and after Morning and Evening Prayer, and also before and after Sermons; and moreover in private houses for their godly solace and comfort . . ..*

But while psalm singing was popular in homes and in some churches, larger cathedrals still preferred the sounds of choirs, sharing their monarch's preferences. Elizabeth was less interested in religious reform than in impressive formality, pleasant music, and sophisticated and elegant homilies. Nor did she care for congregational singing, preferring the sound of organs and trained voices. Services in the Anglican Church greatly resembled those of the Catholic Church, albeit in English rather than Latin. However, those who had tasted the spiritual fervor of Geneva, with its simplicity of form, congregational psalmody, and emphasis on a spiritually conducted life, were determined to bring these transformations to the English church.

Many reformers came to be called Puritans because of their intent to purify the Church of England from within. They believed the true church consisted only of God's elect rather than those who followed a particular creed.

Some dissenters, convinced that it was necessary to withdraw from the established church because of its doctrine and organization, organized themselves into independent congregations of believers (they were called "separatists") and withdrew from fellowship with those who were not redeemed. Many fled England to live in the less religiously restrictive Holland. The Pilgrims who settled Plymouth Colony in 1620 were members of this group. Although separatists used Day's psalter, they were uncomfortable with its liberalism, since the Biblical texts had been changed considerably to accommodate meter, rhyme, and style.

Most of these reformers practiced infant baptism. Others would come to believe that baptism should be administered only to believing adults; among these was the group to be known as the Baptists.

Thus Christians in England were separated into distinctive groups. Those who claimed the established Church of England were, of course, in the majority; they were most agreeable to the Queen and least likely to sing congregationally. Music in larger Anglican churches was provided by choir and organ. In smaller Anglican churches congregations might participate in psalm singing during Morning or Evening Prayers.

Puritans, though often practicing members of the established church, believed that it walked too closely to Rome in its practices. Some of them organized their own religious services, which included congregational psalm singing, scripture reading, preaching, and extemporaneous prayer. They sang psalms loudly and at every opportunity, generally in unison and unaccompanied, to avoid the appearance of "popery" — a term that in Puritan usage applied not only to Catholicism, but also to the dignified rituals of the Church of England. Puritans remained active in British church and political arenas and later, led by Oliver Cromwell, would overthrow and execute Charles I and establish the Commonwealth.

The third of these groups consisted of Separatists, who saw little hope for reforming the Anglican Church and determined to set their own path, largely according to a Calvinist model. Their meetings featured congregational psalm singing, scripture reading, preaching, and prayer. Separatists wielded no political power, and their leaders were often imprisoned for their antiestablishment practices.

So "Sternhold and Hopkins" was used in England by some Anglican choirs, with occasional congregational participation; by Puritan and separatist congregations for their regular meetings; and by all in home and private devotional gatherings. It would be published in scores of editions over a period of three hundred years; for over a century it was the favored psalter of the Anglican Church. Most of its songs have fallen into disuse; one that is still familiar is William Kethe's version of Psalm 100, set to a tune borrowed from the *Genevan Psalter* (in which Calvin and Bourgeois had used it for Psalm 134, PftL 17).

OLD HUNDRED

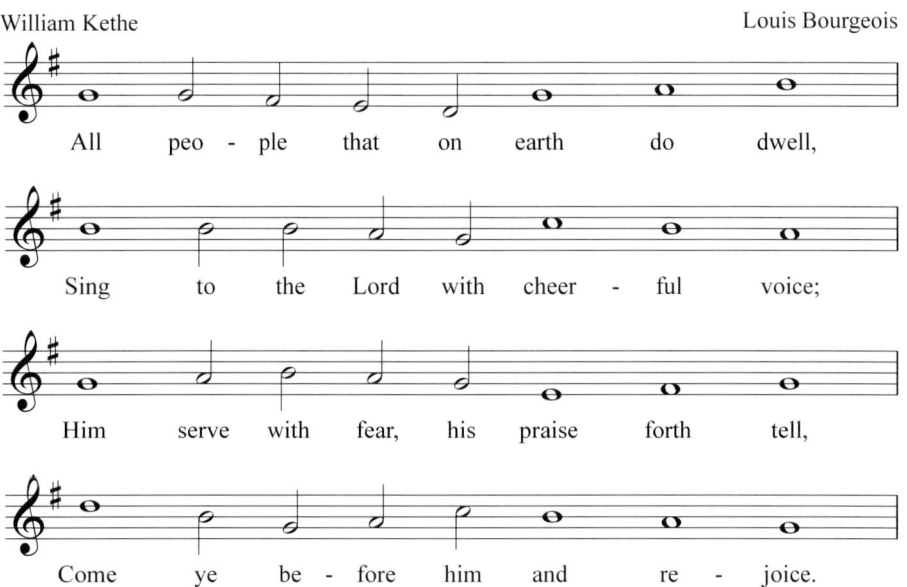

William Kethe   Louis Bourgeois

All peo - ple that on earth do dwell,

Sing to the Lord with cheer - ful voice;

Him serve with fear, his praise forth tell,

Come ye be - fore him and re - joice.

The Lord ye know is God indeed,
without our aid he did us make;
We are his flock, he doth us feed,
and for his sheep he doth us take.

O enter then his gates with praise,
approach with joy his courts unto.
Praise, laud, and bless his Name always,
for it is seemly so to do.

For why? the Lord our God is good,
his mercy is for ever sure;
His truth at all times firmly stood,
and shall from age to age endure.

The Scottish Psalter

One of the leaders of the Marian exiles in Geneva had been John Knox, a Scotsman who had spent some time preaching in England. Returning to Scotland in 1559, he led in the establishment of a Reformed Protestant national church in 1560 and preached at St. Giles' Cathedral in Edinburgh.

Knox was the country's most powerful political and religious figure until his death in 1752. Under his leadership, the *Scottish Psalter* was published in 1564, with seventy-six entries taken directly from Sternhold and Hopkins, others taken from the *Anglo-Genevan Psalter*, and some newly written. The diversity of music is patterned more after the Genevan model than after Day's; many of the book's 105 tunes were French, and only twelve of them were in Ballad Meter.

This psalter went through a number of editions, the most famous appearing in 1650, in which every psalm appeared in a Common Meter setting (although some were also given in alternate versions in different meters). Here are two versions of Psalm 23. The first, from 1564, was adapted from Sternhold and Hopkins; the second appeared in the 1650 edition (PftL 641 and 642, with later tunes).

The Lord is only my support,
and he that doth me feed;
How can I then lack any thing,
whereof I stand in need?

He doth me fold in coats most safe
the tender grass fast by:
And after driv'th me to the streams
which run most pleasantly.

And when I feel myself near lost,
then doth he me home take,
conducting me in his right paths,
even for his own Name's sake.

And though I were even at death's door,
yet would I fear none ill;
For by thy rod, and shepherd's crook

I am comforted still.
Thou hast my table richly deckt
in despite of my foe;
Thou hast my head with balm refresh'd,
my cup doth over-flow;

And finally, while breath doth last,
thy grace shall me defend;
And in the house of God will I
my life for ever spend.
　　　　　—Revised from English Psalter, 1561, in Scottish Psalter, 1564

The Lord's my shepherd, I'll not want.
He makes me down to lie
In pastures green: he leadeth me
the quiet waters by.

My soul he doth restore again;
and me to walk doth make
Within the paths of righteousness,
ev'n for his own name's sake.

Yea, though I walk in death's dark vale,
yet will I fear none ill:
For thou art with me; and thy rod
and staff me comfort still.

My table thou hast furnished
in presence of my foes;
My head thou dost with oil anoint,
and my cup overflows.

Goodness and mercy all my life
shall surely follow me:
And in God's house for evermore
my dwelling-place shall be.
　　　　　—Scottish Psalter, 1650

Other English psalters

Day's was the first of many English psalters. Matthew Parker, the Arch-bishop of Canterbury, published his own around 1567, notable now for the nine musical settings contributed by Thomas Tallis. The eighth of these pieces, in the form of a canon (we might call it a "round"), was used for Psalm 67. An adaptation can be found at PftL 21.

Another of these Tallis pieces would be exposed to a wider audience through Ralph Vaughan Williams' *Fantasia on a Theme by Thomas Tallis*, composed in 1910. This example shows it with Parker's second psalm. Note that the melody was ordinarily in the tenor part, since a male would

Parker's Psalm 2

take the lead in singing. This tune, like others created for psalmody, has irregular rhythms, insuring that it could not be mistaken for a dance tune or a popular song. It was important that church tunes should not sound like "worldly" music.

Not all psalters offered new versifications; some continued to use those of Sternhold and Hopkins, set to new music. William Daman's Psalter of 1579 and Thomas Este's Psalter of 1592 are harmonized, with the melody usually given to the tenor voice. Daman's was published in part books, so that each voice part would have an entire set of psalms. Este's was arranged so that the oversized work could be laid on a table and all four voices could read from it: two parts were printed side-by-side and the other two parts were printed in different orientations so that they could be read from the other sides of the table. Harmonized psalters were popular in homes in a time when music reading was common among those who were educated and when madrigals and other songs were often sung recreationally. Este also introduced the practice of giving names to the tunes in his book; these were usually derived from locations associated with the tunes' origins. Este's Psalter marked the first appearance of the familiar WINCHESTER (PftL 325), shown here with Psalm 23.

Winchester

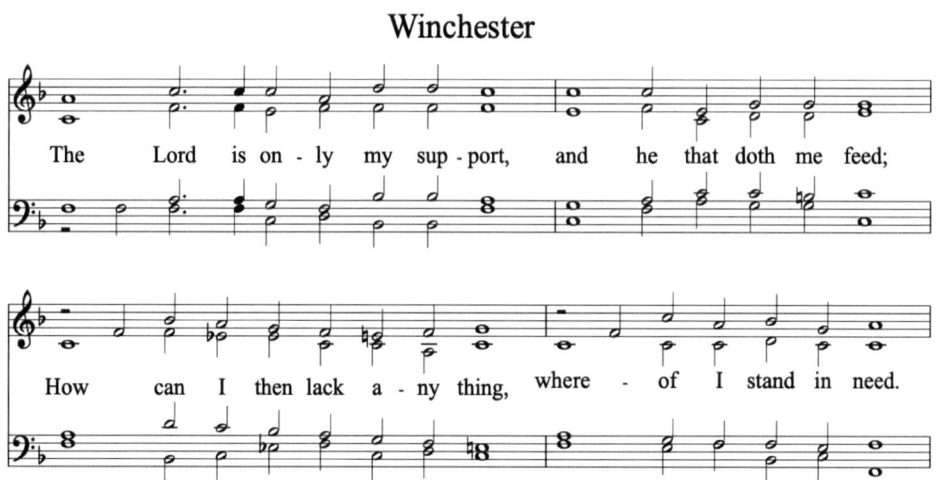

The Lord is on - ly my sup - port, and he that doth me feed;

How can I then lack a - ny thing, where - of I stand in need.

In addition to psalms, other Biblical texts were set metrically for musical presentation. These included the canticles, of course; but there is even an anonymous versification of half of the Acts of the Apostles.

CHAPTER 6

SEVENTEENTH-CENTURY PSALMODY

Thomas Ravenscroft was an editor and a musician who published a notable psalter in 1621:

The Whole Booke of Psalmes: with the Hymnes Evangelicall, and Songs Spirituall. Composed into 4. parts by sundry Authors, to such severall Tunes, as have beene, and are usually sung in England, Scotland, Wales, Germany, Italy, France, and the Nether-lands: Never as yet before in one volume published. Also: 1. A briefe Abstract of the Prayse, Efficacie, and Vertue of the Psalmes. 2. That all Clarkes of Churches, and the Auditory, may know what Tune each proper Psalme may be sung unto. Newly corrected and enlarged by Tho. Ravenscroft Bachelar of Musicke.

The texts were familiar, having come from the Old Version, but the musical settings were new and ambitious. Some of the most famous composers in the country provided harmonizations, almost certainly upon the payment of commissions. The tunes that they harmonized were drawn largely from the common repertoire, but Ravenscroft gave names to most of these tunes (this practice was not completely new), and his pairings of titles and tunes have, in many cases, stuck solidly.

There are twenty-three songs besides the psalms, including canticles, the Ten Commandments, prayers, hymns, and instructive texts. Six of the psalms appear in two different versions. The text for Psalm 119 stretches over five large double pages; to sing it in its entirety, one would have to repeat Giles Farnaby's setting of the unnamed tune eighty-nine times.

Only five of the psalms are given individual tunes. The most popular tune, WINCHESTER, was shared by six psalms, including Psalm 23. Ravenscroft's practice was to print each part separately, on the same page.

The tune DUNDEE (PftL 192) had first appeared in Andro Hart's 1615 Edinburgh Psalter, under the name FRENCH TUNE. Ravenscroft renamed it and used it for Psalms 36 and 90. Here is his Psalm 36.

Ravenscroft's Psalm 36

DUNDEE, harmonized by Ravenscroft

It is with Hart's and Ravenscroft's Psalters that the idea of the "Common" tune began to take hold. Some tunes were "Proper," intended for specific texts and not likely to be used with others. "Common" tunes were not dedicated to a particular text and could be used for any song with the appropriate meter.

Since Ballad Meter was used more than any other, it came to be known as "Common" Meter (8.6.8.6). Later, two other familiar meters would be similarly named: Long Meter (8.8.8.8) and Short Meter (6.6.8.6). The three are often abbreviated CM, LM, and SM. Note that the terms "Common Meter" and "Common Tunes" have different meanings. A Common Tune could be in any meter; a Common Meter tune could be a Proper Tune.

The most highly positioned writer of a psalter was King James I of England (also Scotland's James VI), best known today for authorizing the Bible translation. His psalter was printed in 1631, sixteen years after his death, but its metrical schemes were incompatible with the favored tunes, and it was not widely used. As an example of royal versification, consider his Psalm 1, in 10.10.10.10.8.6.8.6 meter.

That mortal man most happy is and blest
who in the wickeds counsels doth not walk,
nor zit in sunners wayis doth stay and rest
Nor sittis in seats of skornfull men in talk
but contrair fixis his delicht
into Jehouas law
and on his law both day and nicht
to think is never slaw.

He salbe lyk a plesant plantit tree
upon a reuer syde incressing tal,
that yieldis his frute in saison dew, we see;
whose plesant leif doth neuer fade nor fal.
Now this is surely for to say
that quhat he takis in hand,
it sal withoutin doute alway
most prosperously stand.

But wicked men ar nowayis of that band;
but as the caffe quhich be the wind is tost
thairfor they sall not in that jugement stand
nor yett among the iust be sinneris lost.
For gret Jehova cleirly knowis
the iust mans way upricht
but sure the wickeds way that throwis
sall perish be his micht.

John Playford, one of London's premier music printers in mid-century, had published *The English Dancing Master* in 1651. His 1671 psalter broke new ground textually and musically: textually because these books contained some new hymns, each usually appearing after a psalm and to be sung to the psalm's tune; musically because the settings reflected new tastes, and because there were considerable instructions for singing, including an introduction to the fa-sol-la system of music reading.

John's son Henry edited and published his own collection in 1701, introducing new musical settings and designed, as he explained in the Preface, to be bound with his father's psalter:

> *The Divine Companion, or David's Harp new Tun'd. Being a Choice Collection of New and Easy Psalms, Hymns and Anthems. The Words of the Psalms being Collected from the Newest Versions. Compos'd by the best Masters. To be used in Churches or Private Families, for their greater Advancement of Divine Music.*

This supplement included new tunes for some psalms and a few hymns, catering to the new Restoration musical tastes. He included a few works which he called anthems, for the use of those who desired a more challenging musical experience. As Ravenscroft had done eighty years earlier, Playford engaged some of his generation's leading composers for the musical settings. William Croft's music for Psalm 42, designated Anthem XV, is shown on the next page as an example of the new style.

Psalters were not designed for the Anglican liturgy, though some church leaders might choose to use them in their assemblies. On the occasions when congregations sang, it was not assumed that they would be able to read either text or music. In their 1645 *Directory for the Publique Worship of God*, Presbyterians recommended a procedure for the singing of unfamiliar texts. This practice, in which the deacon would read each line, often singing it to the appropriate tune, before it was sung by the congregation, came to be known as "lining out" and was widely used by many religious groups.

The New Version

Even as the Playford publications were providing urbane musical settings to be used in homes and informal gatherings, there was a brief resurgence of interest in traditional psalm tunes in 1696, when Nahum Tate

Anthem XV

Psalm 42

William Croft

and Nicholas Brady produced a psalter that was approved by William III for use in Anglican congregations that elected to use it. Tate, the English Poet Laureate, had been the librettist for Henry Purcell's opera *Dido and Aeneas*; and Brady was chaplain to William, Mary, and Anne.

A series of supplements followed; the one in 1708 included the tunes ST. ANNE (next page, used with Psalm 42) (PftL 470).

Tate and Brady Supplement Psalm 42

Psalm 42

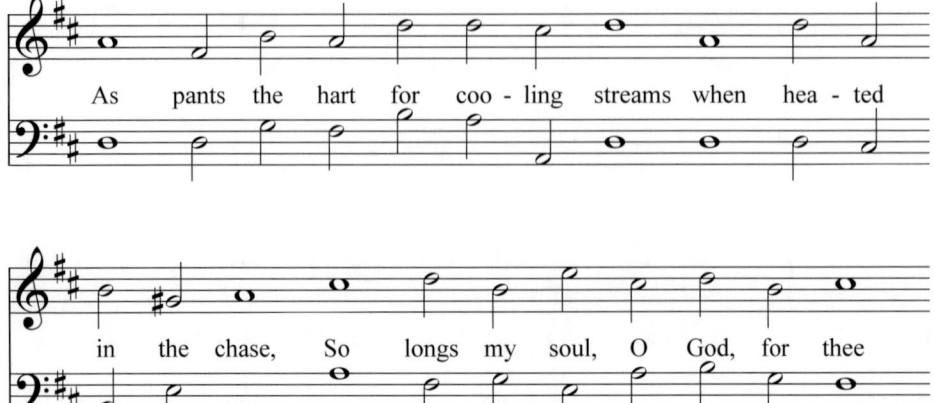

As pants the hart for coo - ling streams when hea - ted

in the chase, So longs my soul, O God, for thee

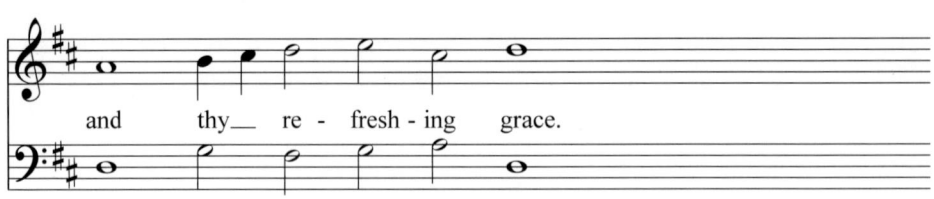

and thy__ re - fresh - ing grace.

and the robust HANOVER, by William Croft.

Tate and Brady Supplement Psalm 149

Psalm 149

William Croft

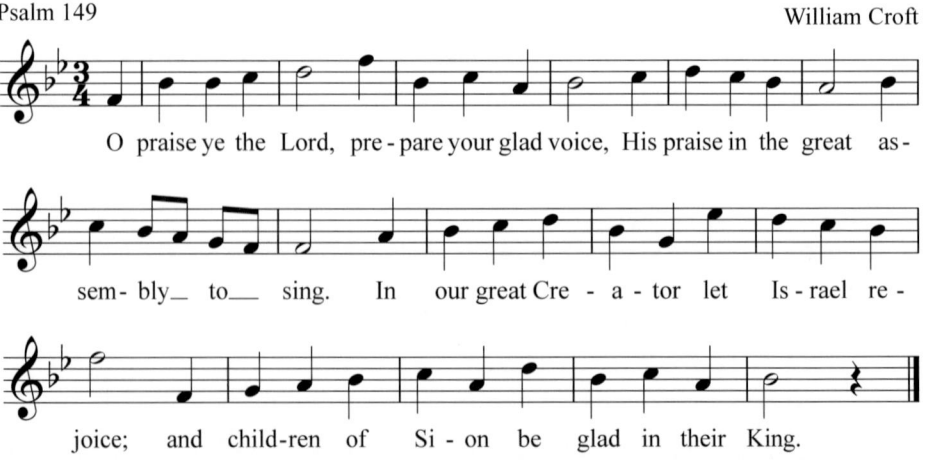

O praise ye the Lord, pre - pare your glad voice, His praise in the great as-

sem- bly__ to__ sing. In our great Cre - a - tor let Is - rael re -

joice; and child-ren of Si - on be glad in their King.

A number of more exuberant tunes were contained in *Lyra Davidica: or, A collection of divine songs and hymns, partly translated from the High-German, and Latin hymns; and set to easy and pleasant tunes, for more general use*, published anonymously in London in 1708. Earlier psalters and hymnals had generally contained melodies that were simple rather than entertaining; this would begin to change during the eighteenth century. "The Resurrection," from *Lyra Davidica*, illustrates this trend toward more complex and engaging music. It is found in a slightly different setting at PftL 97.

Jesus Christ is Risen Today

Lyra Davidica

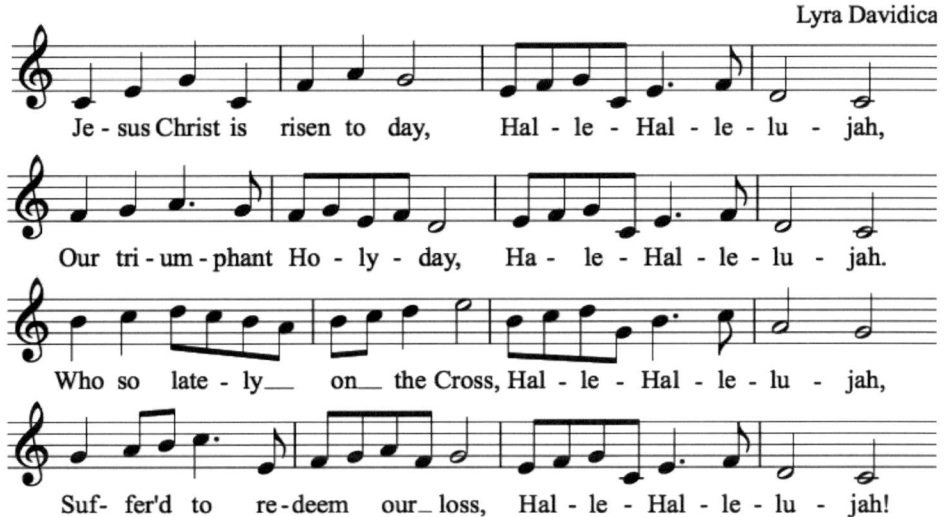

Je - sus Christ is risen to day, Hal - le - Hal - le - lu - jah,

Our tri - um - phant Ho - ly - day, Ha - le - Hal - le - lu - jah.

Who so late - ly on the Cross, Hal - le - Hal - le - lu - jah,

Suf- fer'd to re-deem our loss, Hal - le - Hal - le - lu - jah!

Hest ye females from your fright, Hall. &c.
Take to Galilee your flight; Hall.
To his sad disciples say, Hall.
Jesus Christ is risen to-day. Hall.

In our Paschal joy and feast, Hall.
Let the Lord of life be blest, Hall.
Let the Holy Trine be prais'd, Hall.
And thankful hearts to heaven be rais'd. Hall.

American Psalmody

Henry Ainsworth, a separatist who moved to Holland, joined a group in Amsterdam that was displeased with the liberties that had been taken in the Old Version in order to accommodate rhyme and meter. Acquainted with Hebrew, he made a paraphrase of the psalms in 1612 that came to be widely accepted among dissenters, to the point that it was often bound with the Geneva Bible (a translation that had been completed in 1560 by exiles in Geneva). Accompanying each metrical versification was a prose translation of the psalm. When a group of "Pilgrim" dissenters went to Plymouth in 1620 they carried the Geneva Bible and the Ainsworth Psalter. Ainsworth's *The Book of Psalmes: Englished both in Prose and metre*, contained thirty-nine tunes, many of them Genevan, with their peculiar meters.[1] But the lively tunes, which Elizabeth I had derided as "Genevan jigs" and the artful verses did not wear well with a band of Pilgrims striving for simplicity in worship.

Ten years after the Plymouth colony was established, a group of Puritans seeking religious reform and economic opportunities settled the Massachusetts Bay Colony, bringing with them an assortment of psalters, including Sternhold and Hopkins, Este's, the Genevan, the Dutch (a Dutch translation of the Genevan), and the Ainsworth. None of these had proven particularly satisfactory, and in 1636 a group of "thirty pious and learned Ministers" decided that a new community in a new world required a new psalter.

The *Bay Psalm Book*, the first book to be published in the colonies,[2] appeared in 1640. Its authors were determined to adhere to the original language as closely as possible, and the preface (generally attributed to Richard Mather) explains their purpose:

> *If therefore the verses are not always so smooth and elegant as some may derive or expect; let them consider that Gods Altar needs not our pollishings: Ex. 20. for wee have respected rather a plaine*

---

[1] Referenced in Henry Wadsworth Longfellow's "The Courtship of Miles Standish":
Open wide on her lap lay the well-worn psalm-book of Ainsworth,
Printed in Amsterdam, the words and the music together,
Rough-hewn, angular notes, like stones in the wall of a churchyard,
Darkened and overhung by the running vine of the verses.
Such was the book from whose pages she sang the old Puritan anthem . . .

[2] The first printing press in New England was purchased and imported for this project.

translation, then to smooth our verses with the sweetnes of any para-
phrase, and soe have attended Conscience rather then Elegance, fi-
delity rather then poetry, in translating the hebrew words into english
language, and Davids poetry into english meetre.

Three men were especially active in the versifications: Richard Mather, of
Dorchester, and Thomas Welde and John Eliot, both of Roxbury. Thomas
Shepard, one of the compilers, encouraged them to be literal:

You Roxb'ry Poets, keep clear of the Crime,
Of missing to give us very good Rhime,
And you of Dorchester, your Verses lengthen,
But with the Texts own Words, you will them strengthen.

Perhaps Shepard's quatrain shows why he was not invited to be more
involved in writing the psalm settings.

John Cotton, another of the compilers, later documented some of the
controversies surrounding congregational psalmody in a treatise with a
revealing title:

Singing of Psalmes a Gospel-Ordinance. Or a treatise, wherein are
handled these particulars: 1. Touching the duty it selfe. 2. Touching
the matter to be sung. 3. Touching the singers. 4. Touching the man-
ner of singing. By John Cotton, teacher of the Church at Boston in
New-England. London, Printed for J. R. at the Sunne and Fountaine
in Pauls-Church-yard: and H. A. at the Crowne in Popes-Head-Alley.
1650.

In this book he attempted to refute the arguments on the one hand of those
who felt the Puritans were too restrictive in singing only lyrical scripture;
and on the other hand of more conservative critics who felt that women
and unbelievers should not participate in singing, and, indeed, that no
artifices of melody and poetry were allowable.

No tunes were printed with the earliest editions, but there were instructions that recommended appropriate tunes from Ravenscroft's psalter. In
theory, only six tunes would have sufficed, since only six meters were
used for the entire collection: CM (Common Meter), SM (Short Meter),
LM (Long Meter), LM Six Lines (8.8.8.8.8.8), LMD (Long Meter Dou-
bled — 8.8.8.8.8.8.8.8), and the curiously named HM (Hallelujah Meter
— 6.6.6.6.4.4.4.4).

The book went through several editions and was in use for well over a hundred years, in England and Scotland as well as in the colonies. The third edition (1651), which came to be known as the *New England Psalm Book*, was significantly revised and its poetry improved. The ninth edition (1698), the first to contain music, included thirteen tunes placed in the back of the book, reprinted from John Playford's *Introduction to the Skill of Musick*, along with Playford's instructions for singing.

Here is a setting of Psalm 23 from the first edition, set to one of the tunes in the ninth edition.

New England Psalm Book Psalm 23

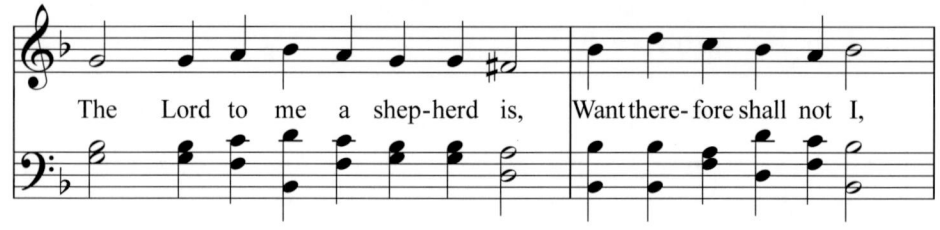

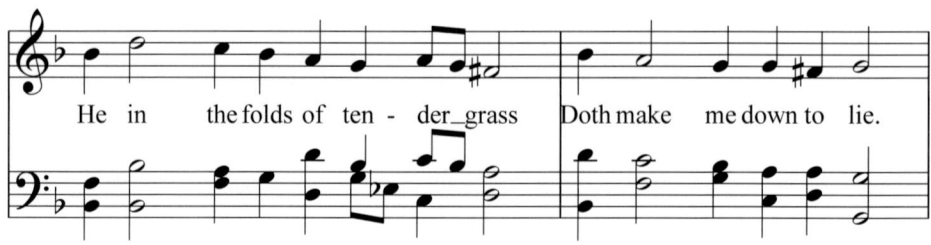

To waters calm he gently leads
Restore my soul doth he
He doth in paths of righteousness
For his names sake lead me.

Yea though in valley of death's shade
I walk none ill I'll fear,
Because thou art with me, thy rod,
and staff my comfort are.

For me a table thou hast spread
In presence of my foes;
Thou dost anoint my head with oil
My cup it over-flows.

Goodness and mercy surely shall
All my days follow me;
And in the Lord's house I shall dwell
So long as days shall be.

Cotton Mather was the grandson of John Cotton and Richard Mather. A noted preacher and a leading figure in the Salem witch trials, he was also interested in congregational song, and in 1718 he produced the *Psalterium Americanum*. Following in the spirit of his grandfathers but desiring to improve upon their work, he wrote in unrhymed verse in order to avoid unnecessary interference in the search for an accurate translation. And he allowed for the choice of either Long or Common Meter tunes for some of the psalms by inserting optional two-syllable words in alternating verses.

My Shepherd is th' Eternal God;
I shall not be in [any] want:
In pastures of a tender grass
He [ever] makes me to lie down:

To waters of tranquilities
He gently carries me [along].
My feeble and my wandering Soul
He [kindly] does fetch back again;

In the plain paths of righteousness
He does lead [and guide] me along,
because of the regard He had
[ever] unto His Glorious Name.

There is no indication that any congregation (including Mather's) adopted his psalter.

CHAPTER 7

EARLY ENGLISH HYMNODY

The few hymns[1] that had appeared in sixteenth- and seventeenth-century psalters were generally considered appropriate for private gatherings but not for church assemblies. Objectors admitted that hymnody had indeed been a part of early church meetings but argued that the practice had been limited to those with a particular spiritual gift. Some believed that only ministers should be allowed to sing hymns, since they were uniquely accepted as God's spokesmen. But ministers were not equally adept, and while they might be expected to extemporize in prayer; few were as successful in improvisational hymn singing. Additionally, many believed that it was a matter of excessive artifice to rhyme texts and impose meter in the utterance of spiritual thoughts (although these devices were usually acknowledged as requirements for psalm singing).

Hymns had been prohibited in English churches by Henry VIII and Cranmer, and Henry rejected Coverdale's *Goostly Psalmes* in 1536. George Wither in 1623 failed to apply for a license when he published *Hymns and Songs of the Church* (even if he had applied, it would not have been granted), and he spent some time in prison for this oversight..

Beginnings of English hymnody

But the English had shown a quiet tolerance for hymnody that accelerated around 1700. Six hymns had been included in Day's Psalter, and more appeared in seventeenth-century publications. The 1708 Supplement to Tate and Brady included sixteen hymns and scriptural versifications, including this paraphrase of Luke 2:8-15 by Tate, published with the tune ST. JAMES.

---

1 Whereas *hymnos* specified songs of praise in Greek, the tern "hymn" is generally used today for texts of various types for congregational singing.

While Shepherds Watched Their Flocks By Night

Nahum Tate

ST. JAMES

While shep-herds watched their flocks by night, all seat-ed on the ground,

the an-gel of the Lord came down, and glo - ry— shone a-round.

*"Fear not!" said he, (for mighty dread
had seized their troubled mind),
"Glad tidings of great joy I bring
to you and all mankind."*

*"To you, in David's town, this day
is born of David's line
the Savior, who is Christ the Lord,
and this shall be the sign:"*

*"The heavenly babe you there shall find
to human view display'd,
all meanly wrapped in swathing bands,
and in a manger laid."*

*Thus spake the seraph, and forthwith
appear'd a shining throng
of Angels, praising God, and thus
address'd their joyful song:*

*"All glory be to God on high,
and to the earth be peace;
good will henceforth, from heaven to men
begin, and never cease."*

The true seedbed of English hymnody was in the separatists, who, in spite of their loyalty to Calvin's teachings (which included a ban on hymnody), favored fewer restrictions on church practices. One of the early leaders was Benjamin Keach, pastor of the Particular Baptist Church in Southwark, who around 1673 instituted the singing of a congregational hymn after the Lord's Supper.[2] Within twenty years Keach had published *Spiritual Melody*, with nearly three hundred hymns. By the end of the century other Baptist groups were following Southwark's lead. Here is one of Keach's poems from 1691, set to a tune Ravenscroft had published seventy years earlier.

How Glorious Are the Morning Stars

They sang together at the first
Jehovah's glorious praise,
And we of them also must learn
To sing to God always;

Nay, with united voices sing
In consort, with much joy,
Since Christ has overcome our Foes,
Who would our souls destroy.

It is his due, and it belongs
To him as his just Right;
His praise to celebrate in songs
Is lovely in his sight.

---

[2] Scriptural authority for this practice was claimed by some, since Matthew 26:30 records that, after the Lord's Supper, "When they had sung a hymn, they went out to the Mount of Olives." Nevertheless, Keach's congregation split over this matter.

Keach's style is not fluid, his tone is more didactic than personal, and his hymns did not attract attention outside of his congregation. But the time was nearing for the popularization of hymns in England. It would require a relaxation of cultural opposition and a compelling author to accelerate the movement, These were to arrive in the early 1700s.

Isaac Watts

It was the work of Isaac Watts (1674-1748) that opened the door to the acceptance of congregational hymn singing in England and America. The  son of a religious dissenter who was imprisoned on numerous occasions for his teaching,[3] Isaac was brought up with a classical education and showed early talent for languages and poetry. Having studied Latin from the time he was four, he began Greek at nine, French at eleven, and Hebrew at thirteen. When he was seven he wrote an acrostic poem that demonstrated poetic promise and Calvinistic conviction:

I am a vile polluted lump of earth;
So I've continued ever since my birth;
Although Jehovah grace does daily give me,
As sure this monster Satan will deceive me.
Come therefore, Lord, from Satan's claws relieve me.

Wash me in thy blood, O Christ,
And grace divine impart;
Then search and try the corners of my heart,
That I in all things may be fit to do
Service to Thee, and sing Thy praises too.

Watt's first hymn was written when he was around sixteen. After attending a morning service, he complained to his father about the generally poor quality of the songs of the congregation. His father told him not to complain unless he could produce better; by that evening Isaac had written an eight-stanza hymn, which was lined out at the close of the evening assembly. It is still sung; here are its opening stanzas.

---

[3] Isaac was born while his father, the Deacon of a Congregational Chapel in Southampton, was in prison, and he was nursed on the building's steps while his parents visited.

Behold the Glories of the Lamb
  Amidst His Father's Throne;
Prepare new Honours for his Name
  And Songs before unknown.

Let Elders worship at his Feet,
  The Church adore around,
With Vials full of Odours sweet,
  And Harps of sweeter sound.

With this hymn he demonstrated the qualities that were to make his works beloved — the easy imagery, the naturalness of language, and, most importantly, the sense that all is scripturally founded (in this case, tied to Revelation 5). From that point, Watts wrote regularly, ultimately producing more than five hundred hymns and psalm adaptations. As a nonconformist, he had no obligation to *The Book of Common Prayer* or to the church calendar for thematic material; if there was any regular source of topical material, it would have been the sermon of the day. For some years those sermons were his own.

He was in his early twenties when he first preached, and in 1694 he was appointed assistant minister to the Independent Church in Mark Lane, London. He served in that position for three years and as minister for ten years until ill health forced him to retire. During this tenure, in 1705, he published *Horae Lyricae*, a collection of hymns and religious poems. It was well received — because of it Samuel Johnson included Watts in his *Lives of the English Poets* — and he was encouraged to follow it with a collection of poems more uniformly suitable for singing.

Hymns and Spiritual Songs (1707) included hymns based on scripture, hymns for the Lord's Supper, and hymns "on divine subjects." With two of these categories he was in relatively safe territory. Writing hymns based on scripture was essentially the same as paraphrasing scripture, and that is what had been done with the psalms for centuries. With these hymns, we are still praising God with "His own words." The second section, hymns connected to the Lord's Supper, were often considered justifiable, since Jesus and his disciples sang a hymn after the original event: "When they had sung a hymn, they went out to the Mount of Olives" (Matt. 26:30).

More questionable were the hymns "on divine subjects." He admitted in his preface to the book that their "Form is of mere humane Composure" but expressed the hope that "the Sense and Materials will always appear Divine." He was largely successful in that aim, and his hymns were to find a popular approval where others' had not. It was their rooting in scripture, and the consequent sense of spiritual authority, that sealed their success. In the magnificent "Christ crucified, the wisdom and power of God," number ten from Part III, Watts expanded his scope to encompass the wonder of God's creative and redemptive work.

Nature with open volume stands,
To spread her Maker's praise abroad;
And every labor of his hands
Shows something worthy of a God.

But in the grace that rescued man
His brightest form of glory shines;
Here, on the cross, 'tis fairest drawn,
In precious blood and crimson lines.

[Here his whole name appears complete;
Nor wit can guess, nor reason prove,
Which of the letters best is writ,
The power, the wisdom, or the love.][4]

Here I behold his inmost heart,
Where grace and vengeance strangely join,
Piercing his Son with sharpest smart,
To make the purchased pleasure mine.

O! the sweet wonders of that cross,
Where God the Savior loved and died
Here noblest life my spirit draws
From his dear wounds and bleeding side.

I would for ever speak his name,
In sounds to mortal ears unknown;
With angels join to praise the Lamb,
And worship at his Father's throne.

---

[4] Watts used brackets on occasion to indicate stanzas that could be omitted without significant loss.

These Lord's Supper hymns have proven to be among his most enduring works. One of his best known intimately ties our own complicity with Jesus' suffering on the cross and is set here to ST. ANNE (PftL 470),

Alas! and Did My Saviour Bleed

Isaac Watts   ST. ANNE

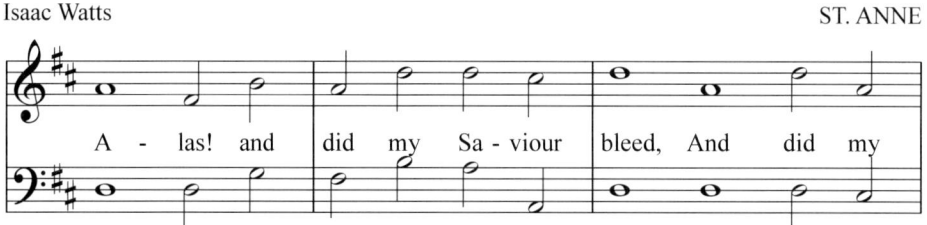

A - las! and did my Sa - viour bleed, And did my

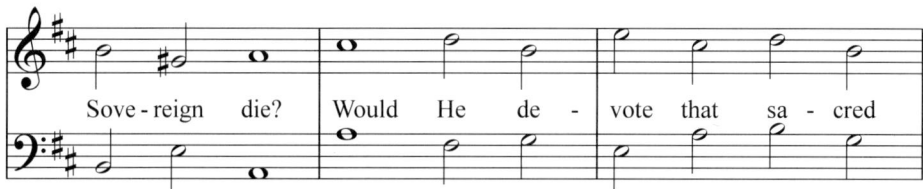

Sove - reign die? Would He de - vote that sa - cred

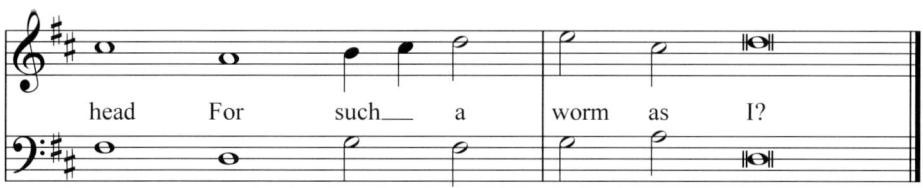

head For such___ a worm as I?

[Thy body slain, sweet Jesus, Thine,
And bathed in its own blood,
While all exposed to wrath divine
The glorious Sufferer stood]

Was it for crimes that I had done
He groaned upon the tree?
Amazing pity! grace unknown!
And love beyond degree!

Well might the sun in darkness hide
And shut his glories in
When Christ, the mighty Maker died
For man the creature's sin

Thus might I hide my blushing face
While His dear cross appears
Dissolve my heart in thankfulness
And melt my eyes to tears

But drops of grief can ne'er repay
The debt of love I owe
Here, Lord, I give my self away
'Tis all that I can do.[5]

The term "worm" (often modified to "one" in modern hymnals) reminds us of Watts' conviction of inherent guilt, the same conviction expressed as a seven year old, when he claimed to be a "vile, polluted lump of earth," or in an entry in a list of significant events in his life noting that when he was fourteen he "fell under considerable conviction of sin."

In 1712, when a chronic fever required him to give up his pulpit, he was invited by one of his parishioners, Sir Thomas Abney (who had been chosen Lord Mayor of London in 1700), to spend a week with him at his estate. Watts accepted — and remained with the family (with their glad consent) thirty-six years until his death.

His next significant publication was *The Psalms of David imitated in the language of the New Testament, and apply'd to the Christian state and worship* (1719), which contained "Jesus Shall Reign Where'er the Sun" (Ps. 72), "Joy to the World" (Ps. 98:4,6-9), and "Our God, Our Help in Ages Past" (Ps. 90). His goal with these 138 versifications was both to "Christianize" and to "Nationalize" the psalms, as in his setting of Psalm 100 (see Charles Wesley's adaptation of this text at PftL 64):

Sing to the Lord with joyful voice,
Let every land his name adore;
The British isles shall send the noise
Across the ocean to the shore.

Nations, attend before his throne
With solemn fear, with sacred joy;
Know that the Lord is God alone;
He can create and he destroy.

---

[5] See PftL 12 for Ralph Hudson's musical setting, with an added refrain, which most certainly would not have had Watts' approval.

His sovereign power, without our aid,
Made us of clay and formed us men;
And when, like wand'ring sheep, we strayed,
He brought us to his fold again.

We are his people, we his care,
Our souls and all our mortal frame:
What lasting honors shall we rear,
Almighty Maker, to thy name?

We'll crowd thy gates with thankful songs,
High as the heav'ns our voices raise;
And earth with her ten thousand tongues
Shall fill thy courts with sounding praise.

Wide as the world is thy command,
Vast as eternity thy love!
Firm as a rock thy truth must stand,
When rolling years shall cease to move.

Convinced that there were some of the psalms that did not easily apply to the Christian's life, Watts did not attempt to set all 150 of them. And some that were especially friendly he versified more than once. Here are two of his three settings of Psalm 23. Note especially the warmth of the concluding lines of the first version (found at PftL 428 with an American pentatonic tune; the second is at PftL 643 with a later American tune).

Psalm 23:2. CM
My Shepherd will supply my need,
Jehovah is his name;
In pastures fresh he makes me feed
Beside the living stream.

He brings my wandering spirit back,
When I forsake his ways;
And leads me for his mercy's sake,
In paths of truth and grace.

When I walk thro' the shades of death,
Thy presence is my stay;
A word of thy supporting breath
Drives all my fears away.

Thy hand, in spite of all my foes,
Doth still my table spread;
My cup with blessings overflows,
Thine oil anoints my head.

The sure provisions of my God
Attend me all my days;
O may thy house be mine abode,
And all my work be praise!

There would I find a settled rest,
(While others go and come)
No more a stranger or a guest,
But like a child at home.

Psalm 23:3. SM
The Lord my shepherd is,
I shall be well supply'd;
Since he is mine, and I am his,
What can I want beside?

He leads me to the place
Where heavenly pasture grows,
Where living waters gently pass,
And full salvation flows.

If e'er I go astray,
He doth my soul reclaim,
And guides me in his own right way,
For his most holy name.

While he affords his aid,
I cannot yield to fear;
Tho' I should walk thro' death's dark shade
My Shepherd's with me there.

In spite of all my foes,
Thou dost my table spread,
My cup with blessings overflows,
And joy exalts my head.

The bounties of thy love
Shall crown my following days;

Nor from thy house will I remove,
Nor cease to speak thy praise.

Watts predominately used the three most familiar meters and on occasion four others. A number of his hymns are still widely sung, including "Am I a Soldier of the Cross?" (PftL 33, 34, 35), "Come, Ye That Love the Lord" (PftL 111, with added refrain), "Come, Let Us Join Our Cheerful Songs" (PftL 105), "How Shall the Young Secure Their Hearts?" (PftL 253), and "I'm Not Ashamed to Own My Lord" (PftL 298).

He and his contemporaries might have heard these songs sung to tunes still in our hymnals, such as the SM tune SOUTHWELL (PftL 393); the CM tunes WINDSOR (PftL 574), WINCHESTER (PftL 325), DUNDEE (PftL 192), (PftL 911), ST. MAGNUS (PftL 639), and ST. ANNE (PftL 470); or the LM tunes OLD HUNDRED (PftL 17), TALLIS' CANON (PftL21), and WAREHAM (PftL 196).

CHAPTER 8

THE WESLEYS AND THEIR SUCCESSORS

A long with the advent of Pietism there was a revival among the *Unitas Fratrum*, the spiritual descendents of John Hus. These disciples had come to be known as Moravians, taking the name of the Czech region in which they had found refuge. In 1722 Count Nikolaus of Zinzendorf (1700-60), the godson of P.J. Spener (the founder of Pietism), invited the Moravians to his estate in Saxony, where they established a settlement called *Herrnhut* ("the Lord's watch"). Zinzendorf led them in instituting the practice of "hours of song," consisting of a sermon followed by the singing (to organ accompaniment) of portions of twenty to thirty hymns chosen to illustrate the topic of the message. During the next thirty years Moravians published thousands of hymns. Zinzendorf's *London Songbook* of 1753 and 1754 included 3,265 hymns in two volumes.

These "hours of song" (German *Singstunden*) offered more than instruction and musical practice. They provided social bonding, motivation, and a common heritage. The Moravians at Herrnhut sent missionaries throughout the world, especially to developing countries, and established Moravian congregations in major population centers. Wherever they went, they took their hymns.

Some of Zinzendorf's hymns, such as "Christian Hearts in Love United," can be found in modern hymnals.

> *Christian hearts, in love united,*
> *Seek alone in Jesus rest;*
> *Has He not your love excited?*
> *Then let love inspire each breast;*

Members on our Head depending
Lights reflecting Him, our Sun,
Brethren His commands attending,
We in Him, our Lord, are one.

Come, then, come, O flock of Jesus,
Covenant with Him anew;
Unto Him Who conquered for us,
Pledge we love and service true;
And should our love's union holy
Firmly linked no more remain,
Wait ye at His footstool lowly,
Till He draw it close again.

Grant, Lord, that with Thy direction,
"Love each other," we comply,
Aiming with unfeigned affection
Thy love to exemplify;
Let our mutual love be glowing,
Thus will all men plainly see,
That we, as on one stem growing,
Living branches are in Thee.

O that such may be our union,
As Thine with the Father is,
And not one of our communion
E'er forsake the path of bliss;
May our light 'fore men with brightness,
From Thy light reflected, shine;
Thus the world will bear us witness,
That we, Lord, are truly Thine.

The Wesleys

John (1703-91) and Charles (1707-88) Wesley, children of Samuel and Susanna Wesley, became two of the most significant religious figures in eighteenth-century England. Samuel was an Anglican clergyman, though he and Susanna both came from Separatist backgrounds, and John followed in his father's steps, enrolling in Christ Church College of Oxford University, graduating in 1724, and being ordained a priest in 1728. He returned to Christ Church in 1729 as a teaching fellow. Charles, now a student, had organized there a small group with the common goal of pursuing a holy life by order and discipline. John assumed the leadership of this "Holy Club," and they developed a required regimen of study, service, and fasting. Outsiders, claiming to find their attempt to be "righteous by method," offended by the implication that members of the Club sought to be more spiritually developed than others who followed the state religion, and perhaps resentful of the implication that they should find similar commitment, disdainfully called the group "Methodists."

John was persuaded by James Oglethorpe, Governor of Georgia, to move to the colony as a minister to the colonists and missionary to the Indians. Charles accepted holy orders in order to join him, and they set sail in October of 1735. Knowing that a group of twenty-six Moravians would also be on the ship, John began to study German in order to be able to converse with them. He continued his study on the journey, using Zinzendorf's newly published *Das Gesang-Buch der Gemeine in Herrnhut* ("The Songbook of the Herrnhut Community") as his text.

Any three-and-a-half-month sea voyage is bound to be eventful; but one could scarcely have foreseen the impact that this journey would have on congregational singing in England and in America.

John was increasingly impressed with the fervor and sincerity of the Moravians, particularly after an event recorded in his Journal, from Sunday, January 25, 1736:

> *In the midst of the psalm wherewith their service began, the sea broke over, split the mainsail in pieces, covered the ship, and poured in between the decks, as if the great deep had already swallowed us up. A terrible screaming began among the English. The Germans calmly sang on. I asked one of them afterward, "Were you not afraid?" He answered, "I thank God, no." I asked, "But were not your women and children afraid?" He replied, mildly, "No; our women and children are not afraid to die."*

Intrigued by this religious community, John developed an interest in their hymns and to translate some of them.[1] In 1737 he published *A Collection of Psalms and Hymns* in Charleston, the first hymnal used in an Anglican Church, and the first hymnal published in America. In addition to five translated Moravian hymns, it included thirty-five Watts hymns, which he altered in order to avoid excessive emotionalism, length, and nationalism. His parishioners did not react favorably to the introduction of hymns into their assemblies. And John encountered other difficulties, not the least of which involved his relationship with a young parishioner who declined his offers of marriage and filed charges of defamation when he banned her from the communion service.

Charles, unable to deal with the situation, returned to England after several months. John followed him in December of 1737, fleeing lest the authorities take him into custody for the legal accusation by the young lady. The brothers' ministry in the colonies had been less than auspicious.

But their contact with the Moravian people and their hymns was life changing. John, challenged by the Germans' claim to a "personal knowledge" of God, expressed his own developing desire for a similar experience in the first of their songs he translated:

> *O God, Thou bottomless abyss,*
> *Thee to perfection who can know?*
> *O height immense! What words suffice,*
> *Thy countless attributes to show?*
>
> *Unfathomable depths Thou art!*
> *O, plunge me in Thy mercy's sea;*
> *Void of true wisdom is my heart,*
> *With love embrace and cover me.*
>
> *While Thee, all-infinite I set,*
> *By faith before my ravish'd eye,*
> *My weakness bends beneath the weight;*
> *O'erpower'd I sink, I faint, I die.*

---

[1] His previous contacts with hymns had not been in Anglican services, where they were practically non-existent, but as a child at devotional gatherings held by his mother for servants and children.

On their return to England they established contact with a group of Moravians that met in a chapel on Aldersgate Street. Each of them claimed a spiritual reawakening or "conversion" in one of these meetings — Charles on May 21, 1738, and John three days later. John traveled to Herrnhut, where he shared with Zinzendorf's community in study, fellowship, and prayer.[2] The brothers' next publication came in 1738: *A Collection of Psalms and Hymns*, which drew heavily from Watts, as had the Charleston collection.

Charles was the poet of the pair, publishing more than four thousand hymns (with or without music) and leaving another three thousand in manuscript. The first of these, "Where Shall My Wondering Soul Begin," was written shortly after his "conversion" on Pentecost of 1738. The following year he produced a hymn on the anniversary of that event, which he titled "For the Anniversary Day of One's Conversion." John suggested that stanzas 7-10, 12-14, 17, and 18 were appropriate for congregational singing, and some or all of these are found in modern hymnals (see PftL 467 and 468). Other verses have been left by the wayside for reasons that are more or less obvious.

> *Glory to God, and praise and love*
> *be ever, ever given,*
> *by saints below and saints above,*
> *the church in earth and heaven.*
>
> *On this glad day the glorious Sun*
> *of Righteousness arose;*
> *on my benighted soul he shone*
> *and filled it with repose.*
>
> *Sudden expired the legal strife,*
> *'twas then I ceased to grieve;*
> *my second, real, living life*
> *I then began to live.*
>
> *Then with my heart I first believed,*
> *believed with faith divine,*
> *power with the Holy Ghost received*
> *to call the Savior mine.*

---

[2] John would later become disaffected with the Moravians, fearing that their spiritual fervor transcended their doctrinal soundness.

I felt my Lord's atoning blood
close to my soul applied;
me, me he loved, the Son of God,
for me, for me he died!

I found and owned his promise true,
ascertained of my part,
my pardon passed in heaven I knew
when written on my heart.

O for a thousand tongues to sing
my dear Redeemer's praise!
The glories of my God and King,
the triumphs of his grace.

My gracious Master and my God,
assist me to proclaim,
to spread through all the earth abroad
the honors of thy name.

Jesus! the name that charms our fears,
that bids our sorrows cease;
'tis music in the sinner's ears,
'tis life, and health, and peace!

He breaks the power of canceled sin,
he sets the prisoner free;
his blood can make the foulest clean;
his blood availed for me.

He speaks, and listening to his voice
new life the dead receive;
the mournful, broken hearts rejoice,
the humble poor believe.

Hear him, ye deaf, his praise, ye dumb,
your loosened tongues employ;
ye blind, behold your Savior come,
and leap, ye lame, for joy.

Look unto him, ye nations, own
your God, ye fallen race!
Look, and be saved through faith alone,
be justified by grace!

See all your sins on Jesus laid;
the Lamb of God was slain,
his soul was once an offering made
for every soul of man.

Harlots and publicans and thieves,
in holy triumph join!
Saved is the sinner that believes
from crimes as great as mine.

Murderers and all ye hellish crew,
ye sons of lust and pride,
believe the Savior died for you;
for me the Savior died.

Awake from guilty nature's sleep,
and Christ shall give you light,
cast all your sins into the deep,
and wash the Ethiop white.

With me, your chief, you then shall know,
shall feel your sins forgiven;
anticipate your heaven below
and own that love is heaven.

This, along with other poems by Charles and others, was published in the Wesleys' *Hymns and Sacred Poems* (1739, 1740, 1742).

Charles's talent at writing poetry that sounds thoroughly scriptural is seen in this familiar "Hymn for Christmas Day" from the 1739 collection, usually sung as adapted by Whitefield and others. The hymn, a true encapsulation of the gospel message, reminds us that the incarnation is an ongoing process, beginning with Jesus' becoming man and continuing with our welcoming him to live in our own hearts, being clothed in our flesh.[3]

Hark how all the Welkin rings
"Glory to the King of Kings,"
Peace on earth, and mercy mild,
God and sinners reconciled!

---

[3] This song is found at PftL 202, unfortunately with an unintended repetition of one of Wesley's stanzas.

Joyful all ye nations rise,
Join the triumph of the skies,
Universal nature say,
"Christ the Lord is born today!"

Christ, by highest Heav'n adored,
Christ, the everlasting Lord,
Late in time behold him come,
Offspring of a virgin's womb.

Veiled in flesh, the Godhead see,
Hail th'incarnate Deity!
Pleased as man with men t'appear
Jesus our Immanuel here!

Hail the Heav'nly Prince of Peace!
Hail the Son of Righteousness!
Light and life to all he brings,
Ris'n with healing in his wings.

Mild he lays his glory by;
Born that man no more may die,
Born to raise the sons of earth,
Born to give them second birth.

Come, desire of nations, come,
Fix in us thy humble home,
Rise, the woman's conqu'ring seed,
Bruise in us the serpent's head.

Now display thy saving pow'r,
Ruin'd nature now restore,
Now in mystic union join
Thine to ours, and ours to thine.

Adam's likeness, Lord, efface,
Stamp thy image in its place,
Second Adam from above,
Reinstate in us thy love.

Let us Thee, though lost, regain
Thee, the life, the Heav'nly man;
O! to all Thyself impart,
Form'd in each believing heart.

Though Charles continued to favor Common, Long, and Short Meters, he used more than thirty meters. Some of his most popular poems include "And Can It Be That I Should Gain," "Christ the Lord Is Risen Today" (PftL 97), "Jesus, Lover of My Soul" (PftL 364, 365), "Love Divine, All Loves Excelling" (PftL 405), "O for a Thousand Tongues to Sing" (taken from his "anniversary" hymn), and "Soldiers of Christ, Arise!" (PftL 585).

John wrote and translated a few hymns, but his greater gifts were in preaching and administration. After 1739 much of his preaching was outside of Anglican assemblies, to the unchurched, and the fellowship that would be called the Methodist Church was formed. In 1743 he began publishing rules for the societies of his converts.

The *Foundery Collection*[4] (1742) is the Wesleys' first publication of hymn tunes, forty-three of them, including HANOVER, TALLIS' CANON, and a barely recognizable AMSTERDAM (John's skills in music notation were limited). The publication gave opening stanzas and melodies; John had misgivings about singing in harmony.[5] Users were directed to the *Hymns and Sacred Poems* collections to find the complete hymn texts. A later publication, *Select Hymns with Tunes Annext* (1761), contained the tunes (with no harmony) in an appendix. By 1780, with the publication of *Sacred Harmony*, John's objections to harmony had lessened to a degree that allowed him to include bass lines and occasional alto lines. His *Pocket Hymn-book for the use of Christians of all Denominations* (1785) included revised suggestions for pairing specific tunes with specific texts, suggestions which were generally followed by later Methodist compilers. In all, the brothers produced sixty-four separate collections of hymns, the most comprehensive being *A Collection of Hymns for the Use of the People called Methodists* in 1780.

Some of Charles Wesley's hymns were openly evangelical, leading to the introduction and popularization of "invitation" songs. Many celebrated the joy of a faithful and believing life. These would be welcomed by the societies and their lay preachers, who were often subjected to persecution for proclaiming doctrine that did not jibe with that of the established church.

---

[4] This collection was named for a building in Finsbury Square, London, formerly used for the manufacture of armaments, damaged in an explosion, and acquired by John for use as Methodist headquarters for nearly forty years.

[5] *A Collection of Tunes Set to Music, As they are commonly Sung at the Foundery*, London: A. Pearson, 1742.

Charles explored other territory in his poetry. Although "Wrestling Jacob" is based firmly on an incident from scripture, it is self-consciously rhapsodic, as an unnamed adversary is revealed to be a savior; and as a repeated mantra — " Wrestling I will not let Thee go / Till I Thy name, Thy nature know" — gives way to the recognition of the stranger's identity.

He experimented with refrains in poems such as "Rejoice, the Lord is King," "Lamb of God, whose bleeding Love," and "Faint is my Head and sick my Heart." But refrains would not be a common feature of his hymns.

John and Charles fell apart from each other after the middle of the century. John continued to be the Methodists' chief editor and administrator, expressing some of the impatience of a father whose children develop practices with which he is not sympathetic. He preferred relatively austere music which served the text and was not in favor of instrumental accompaniment in church meetings.[6] As some of the societies became more enamored of lively and rhythmic tunes, he sought to call them back to earlier practices. In the *Minutes* of 1768 is recorded his admonition:

> *Beware of formality[7] in singing, or it will creep upon us unawares. "Is it not creeping in already," said they, "by these complex tunes which it is scarcely possible to sing with devotion?" Such is "Praise the Lord, ye blessed ones;" such the long quavering hallelujah annexed to the morning song tune, which I defy any man living to sing devoutly. The repeating of the same word so often, as it shocks all common sense, so it necessarily brings in dead formality, and has no more religion in it than a Lancashire hornpipe. Besides that, it is a flat contradiction to our Lord's command, "Use not vain repetitions." For what is vain repetition, if this is not? What end of devotion does it serve? Again, do not suffer the people to sing too slow. This naturally tends to formality, and is brought in by those who have very strong or very weak voices. Is it not possible that all the Methodists in the nation should sing equally quick?*

---

[6] Adam Clarke (c.1760-1832), the Methodist writer and disciple of Wesley, reported in his Commentary (Vol. 4, p. 685), "The late and venerable and most eminent divine, the Rev. John Wesley, who was a lover of music, and an elegant poet, when asked his opinion of instruments of music being introduced into the chapels of the Methodists, said in his terse and powerful manner, 'I have no objections to instruments of music in our chapels, provided they are neither heard nor seen.' I say the same."

[7] "Formality" refers to features that draw attention to form rather than content; in this case, to musical experience rather than textual content.

John included these instructions in his preface to *Sacred Melody* (1761):

1. *Learn these tunes before you learn any others; afterwards learn as many as you please.*
2. *Sing them exactly as they are printed here without altering or mending them at all; and if you have learned to sing them otherwise, unlearn it as soon as you can.*
3. *Sing all. See that you join with a congregation as frequently as you can, let not a slight degree of weariness hinder you. If it is a cross to you take it up and you will find it a blessing.*
4. *Sing lustily and with good courage. Beware of singing as if you were half dead, or half asleep; but lift up your voice with strength. Be no more afraid of your voice, nor more ashamed of its being heard, than when you sung the songs of Satan.*
5. *Sing modestly. Do not bawl, so as to be heard above or distinct from the rest of the congregation so that you may not destroy the harmony; but strive to unite your voice together so as to make one clear melodious sound.*
6. *Sing in time. Whatever time is sung be sure to keep with it, do not run before or stay behind it; but attend close to the leading voices, and move therewith exactly as you can; and take care not to sing too slow. This drawling way naturally steals on all who are lazy, and it is high time to drive it out from us, and sing all our tunes just as quick as we did at first.*[8]
7. *Above all sing spiritually. Have an eye to God in every word you sing. Aim at pleasing him more than yourself or any other creature. In order to do this attend strictly to the sense of what you sing, and*

---

[8] These instructions echo those of Niceta of Remesiana (d. ca. 414), nearly fourteen centuries earlier, in his homily titled *On the usefulness of hymns*: "Thus, beloved, let us sing with alert senses and a wakeful mind, as the psalmist exhorts: 'Because God is king of all the earth,' he says, 'sing ye wisely,' so that a psalm is sung not only with the spirit, that is, the sound of the voice, but with the mind also, and so that we think of what we sing rather than allow our mind, seized by extraneous thoughts as is often the case, to lose the fruit of our labor. One must sing with a manner and melody befitting holiness; it must not proclaim theatrical distress but rather exhibit Christian simplicity in its very musical movement; it must not remind one of anything theatrical, but rather create compunction in the listeners. Further, our voice ought not be dissonant but consonant. One ought not to drag out the singing while another cuts it short, and one ought not to sing too low while another raises his voice. Rather each should strive to integrate his voice within the sound of the harmonious chorus and not project it outwardly in the manner of a cithara as it to make an immodest display. ... And for him who is not able to blend and fit himself in with the others, it is better to sing in a subdued voice than to make a great noise, for thus he performs both his liturgical action and avoids disturbing the singing brotherhood."

see that your heart is not carried away with the sound, but offered to God continuously; so shall your singing be such as the Lord will approve here, and reward you when he cometh in the clouds of heaven.

George Whitefield

One of the Wesleys' close associates in the Holy Club and in their mission to Georgia had been George Whitefield (1714-70), but he disagreed with their Arminian theology and pursued his own work. A powerful preacher, he traveled throughout England and made seven journeys of the colonies from Boston to Savannah, often preaching outdoors because church buildings would not contain the crowds he attracted. He became one of the most recognizable figures of his time in the Colonies. Whitefield emphasized the singing of psalms and hymns and published in 1757 the *Collection of Hymns for Social Worship* for use at his Tabernacle at Moorfields, in London. It was followed a year later by a tunebook, *The Divine Musical Miscellany*. He antagonized the Wesleys by changing the texts of their hymns in order to accommodate his own doctrines, but his hymnbook was tremendously popular and went through thirty-six editions.

His associate in America was Jonathan Edwards, a Puritan preacher, whose "Sinners in the Hand of an Angry God" (1741) became one of the most famous sermons of the century. These men, particularly Whitefield, were the driving force of a period of religious fervor known as the "Great Awakening." Benjamin Franklin would later comment on the breadth of this movement in his autobiography when he wrote that in Philadelphia in 1739 "one could not walk through the town in an evening without hearing psalms sung in different families in every street."

Many denominations firmly opposed the introduction of hymns — but those most touched by the Great Awakening were somewhat receptive, and the words of Isaac Watts and Charles Wesley began to be heard in American churches.

Later hymnody

The Anglican Church continued officially to resist congregational hymnody on two counts: hymns had no place in *The Book of Common Prayer*; and most music was presented by the choir, at least in larger churches.

But Watts and Wesley had showed that hymns could speak compellingly in independent congregations, and other poets soon followed their lead. Indeed, some Anglican congregations were forced to include a bit of congregational hymnody in their assemblies in order to prevent further defection to independent churches, where the singing had proven to be a popular attraction.

During the late eighteenth century many tried their hand at hymn writing. John Cennick (1718-55), a preacher and poet affiliated in turn with the Wesleys, Whitefield, and the Moravians is best remembered today for "Jesus, My All, to Heaven Is Gone," "Children of the Heavenly King" (PftL 87), and "Lo! He Comes with Clouds Descending" (PftL 406). Robert Robinson (1735-90), a Methodist minister before becoming a Baptist pastor, wrote "Come, Thou Fount of Every Blessing" (PftL 500) in 1758.

Though not known as a writer herself, Selina, Countess of Huntingdon (1707-91), had a catalytic effect on the spread of hymnody among Anglicans. A follower of Whitefield, she was a patroness who established sixty-four churches and founded the Countess of Huntingdon Connexion, which separated from the Anglican church in 1781. Wealthy and influential, she counted among her friends and associates Edward Perronet ("All Hail the Pow'r of Jesus' Name," PftL 19 and 20), Phillip Doddridge ("Grace! 'Tis a Charming Sound," PftL 199), George Frideric Handel, and Augustus Toplady ("Rock of Ages," PftL 557); as well as Watts and the Wesleys. In addition to providing funds for hymnists and composers, she edited hymnals and wrote some tunes.

One of her enduring contributions was the commissioning of a tune by Felice de Giardini (1716-96) to be used with the anonymous text "Come, Thou Almighty King" (PftL 100). Giardini's ITALIAN HYMN was first published under the title "An Hymn to the Trinity" in a collection of hymns for the Lock Hospital in 1769. Although sometimes altered in contemporary hymnals, its original form was a clear statement of Trinitarian doctrine:

> Come, thou almighty King,
> help us thy name to sing,
> help us to praise!
> Father all glorious,
> o'er all victorious,
> come and reign over us, Ancient of Days!

Come, thou incarnate Word,
gird on thy mighty sword,
our prayer attend!
Come, and thy people bless,
and give thy word success,
Spirit of holiness, on us descend!

Come, holy Comforter,
thy sacred witness bear
in this glad hour.
Thou who almighty art,
now rule in every heart,
and ne'er from us depart, Spirit of power!

To thee, great One in Three,
eternal praises be,
hence, evermore.
Thy sovereign majesty
may we in glory see,
and to eternity love and adore!

One of the best of the hymn collections from the latter part of the eighteenth century was *A Selection of Hymns from the best authors*, published in 1787 by the Baptist John Rippon. Another Baptist, John Fawcett (1740-1817), is today remembered for his texts "Blest Be the Tie That Binds" (PftL 76) and "Lord, Dismiss Us with Thy Blessing" (PftL 409, 410).

William Shrubsole's MILES LANE (on the next page) represents a breed of congregational song with choral aspirations. It first appeared in *The Gospel Magazine* (1779) with Perronet's "All Hail the Pow'r of Jesus' Name!" with which it is still commonly paired in England, though not in the United States.

The Olney Hymns

Though Anglican churches continued to be closed to hymnody, hymns gained popularity in private prayer and devotional meetings. "Unofficial" hymnals were printed for such occasions. The best of these was the *Olney Hymns* (pronounced "oh-nee") of John Newton (1725-1807) and William Cowper (pronounced "Cooper," 1731-1800). The outline of Newton's life is well known. Having deserted from the British Navy as a youth, he was

All Hail the Pow'r of Jesus' Name

brought back to England through the devices of his father. It was as the captain of a slaving ship that he began a journey back to a faith that ultimately led to his ordination as an Anglican priest and his assignment to the curacy in the village of Olney in Buckinghamshire.[9]

William Cowper settled in Olney in 1767. A respected poet who struggled with bouts of depression (or "melancholia") he found a friend and companion in Newton, and the two discovered and developed their common interest in hymns.

___

[9] One of Newton's finest accomplishments would be his successful counsel to the young William Wilberforce to use his political position as a tool against the institution of slavery; largely as a result of Wilberforce's work, the slave trade was outlawed in 1807 (the year of Newton's death) and slavery was abolished in England in 1833 (the year of Wilberforce's death).

The hymnal that Newton published in 1779 was divided into three sections: *Book I. On select Texts of Scripture*; *Book II. On occasional Subjects*; and *Book III. On the Progress and Changes of the Spiritual Life*. In his introduction he explained that his collaborator had been forced "by a long and affecting indisposition" to curtail his work. Consequently, the bulk of the collection (281 poems) was from his pen, while sixty-seven poems were from Cowper. The book contained no tunes.

Some of Cowper's hymns express a longing for contentment. An example from the first book, under the heading "Walking with God. Gen 5:24," is this familiar text (PftL 461).

> *O! for a closer walk with God,*
> *A calm and heav'nly frame;*
> *A light to shine upon the road*
> *That leads me to the Lamb!*
>
> *Where is the blessedness I knew*
> *When first I saw the LORD?*
> *Where is the soul–refreshing view*
> *Of JESUS, and his word?*
>
> *What peaceful hours I once enjoyed!*
> *How sweet their memory still!*
> *But they have left an aching void,*
> *The world can never fill.*
>
> *Return, O holy Dove, return,*
> *Sweet messenger of rest;*
> *I hate the sins that made thee mourn,*
> *And drove thee from my breast.*
>
> *The dearest idol I have known,*
> *Whate'er that idol be;*
> *Help me to tear it from thy throne,*
> *And worship only thee.*
>
> *So shall my walk be close with God,*
> *Calm and serene my frame;*
> *So purer light shall mark the road*
> *That leads me to the Lamb.*

Another of Cowper's contributions, from Book 3 (PftL 192), titled "Light shining out of darkness," finds assurance in the midst of difficulties.

God moves in a mysterious way,
  His wonders to perform;
He plants his footsteps in the sea,
  And rides upon the storm.

Deep in unfathomable mines
  Of never failing skill
He treasures up his bright designs,
  And works his sovereign will.

Ye fearful saints fresh courage take,
  The clouds ye so much dread
Are big with mercy, and shall break
  In blessings on your head.

Judge not the LORD by feeble sense,
  But trust him for his grace;
Behind a frowning providence,
  He hides a smiling face.

His purposes will ripen fast,
  Unfolding every hour;
The bud may have a bitter taste,
  But sweet will be the flow'r.

Blind unbelief is sure to err, Jn 8:7
  And scan his work in vain;
GOD is his own interpreter,
  And he will make it plain.

Newton's texts include "Glorious Things of Thee Are Spoken" (PftL 165) and "How Sweet the Name of Jesus Sounds" (PftL 256, 257). But the enduring favorite is "Amazing Grace," from Book 1, under the heading "Faith's review and expectation" and paired with I Chronicles 17:16,17.

Amazing grace! (how sweet the sound)
  That saved a wretch like me!
I once was lost, but now am found,
  Was blind, but now I see.

'Twas grace that taught my heart to fear,
And grace my fears relieved;
How precious did that grace appear,
The hour I first believed!

Through many dangers, toils and snares,
I have already come;
'Tis grace has brought me safe thus far,
And grace will lead me home.

The LORD has promised good to me,
His word my hope secures;
He will my shield and portion be,
As long as life endures.

Yes, when this flesh and heart shall fail,
And mortal life shall cease,
I shall possess, within the veil,
A life of joy and peace.

The earth shall soon dissolve like snow,
The sun forbear to shine;
But GOD, who called me here below,
Will be for ever mine.

Newton probably had no particular tune in mind when he wrote these words. He certainly never heard them sung to the tune that we now associate with the poem (NEW BRITAIN, PftL 36), since it did not appear until after his death. Likewise, the verses now commonly added to Newton's poem — beginning "When we've been there ten thousand years" — were the later product of an anonymous author.

Olney Hymns documented the developing popularity of hymnody among Anglicans, in informal gatherings if not in the liturgy. Congregational hymn singing had been established on the continent by Hussites, Lutherans, and Anabaptists, and hymns were central to Zinzendorf's gatherings. In Britain, Watts provided reason for reconsidering the objections to hymnody, and the popularity of the Wesleyan movement and its hearty congregational singing encouraged a more widespread participation.

Chapter 9

American Hymnody and Singing Schools

I n the early eighteenth century congregational singing was in a sorry state in the colonies. Most tunes were "lined out" by a leader, and singing was often inaccurate, extremely slow, unmusical, and competitive; musical illiteracy prevailed. A number of reformers sought to restore "singing by note" rather than "singing by rote," or "regular singing" as opposed to "common singing." In 1721 John Tufts published in Massachusetts *An Introduction to the Singing of Psalm-Tunes*, the first of many singing school manuals. Rather than traditional musical notation, his tunes were written with F, S, L, and M, the first letters of the syllables representing notes of the scale, as in this printing of WESTMINSTER from the 1727 edition, with its transcription.

The clergyman Cotton Mather (1663-1728) promoted singing schools and musical literacy and claimed that over a three-year period the churches of Boston had been brought to a state of regular singing. But there were those who strongly and vocally preferred the old practice. In 1720 Reverend T. Symmes, of Bradford, a supporter of singing by note, facetiously summarized "all Objections I could remember to have heard about this matter:

1. That is a *new way*, an *unknown tongue*.
2. That it is not so *melodious* as the *usual way*.
3. That there are too *many tunes*, we shall never have done learning.
4. That the practice of it *gives disturbance*; rails and exasperates men's spirits, grieves sundry people, and causes them to behave themselves indecently and disorderly.
5. That it is *Quakerish* and *Popish*, and introductive of *instrumental music*.
6. That the names given to the notes are *bawdy*, yea *blasphemous*.
7. That it is a *needless way*, cause the good Fathers that were strangers to it are got to heaven without it."

One of his colleagues quoted an objection to the effect that regular singing must be wrong because it is favored by young people; and they are unlikely to be supportive of anything that is good![1]

The instructional tunebooks that were produced for singing schools were often horizontally rectangular in shape and contained only one stanza of text for each tune. James Lyon's *Urania* (1761) was an important publication in that it included four-part settings (rather than the more common two- or three-part settings). Among its contents were samples of anthems, plain tunes, and fuging psalm tunes from English parish churches, where the Wesleyan influence had produced new music for spirited singing.

By the early 1800s, tunebooks were using shape notes.[2] Here is OLD HUNDRED as it appeared in Andrew Law's *The Musical Primer* of 1803, published in Cambridge, Massachusetts.

O L D 100 No. 51.

---

[1] Griggs, "The Church Music of Two Centuries," p. 70.

[2] Notes printed as circles, rectangles, triangles, and other shapes, according to the degree of the scale they represented. A number of different systems of shapes have been used.

Billings and fuging tunes

To see that the new tunebooks were put to proper use, itinerant musical reformers began teaching in traveling singing schools. Among the best known of these was William Billings (1746-1800), who published *The New England Psalm Singer* and other collections, conducted many singing schools, and wrote fuging tunes and other compositions. Billings was a colorful figure, blind in one eye and addicted to snuff, with a deformed arm and leg and a harsh voice. He left formal schooling when he was fourteen because of his father's death and made his living as a tanner. But he was a talented self-taught musician, the first American to establish a reputation as a composer, and his works are still performed. One of his most popular tunes is a simple round:

When Jesus Wept

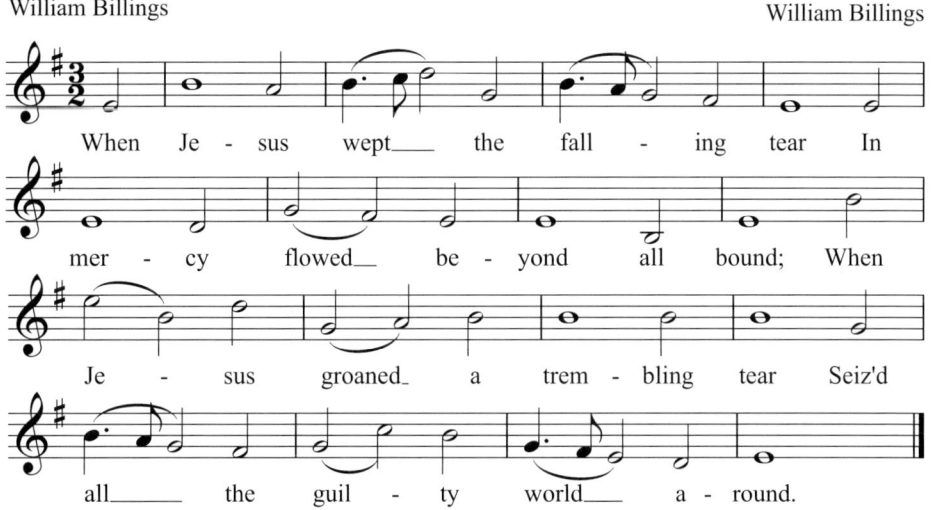

The evangelical fervor spread by the preachers of the Great Awakening had helped to bond the colonies, and many considered the movement toward independence, though violent and bloody, to be providentially ordained,. Billings' CHESTER, conflating providence and patriotism, portrays British anti-revolutionary efforts as futile attempts to thwart the will of "New England's God."

Chester

William Billings   William Billings

Let ty-rants shake their i - ron rod, And Sla-v'ry clank her

gall - ing chains. We fear them not, we trust in

God. New Eng-land's God for e - ver reigns.

Howe and Burgoyne and Clinton too,
With Prescot and Cornwalis join'd.
Together plot our Overthrow,
In one Infernal league conbin'd.

When God inspir'd us for the fight,
Their ranks were broke, their lines were forc'd.
Their Ships were Shatter'd in our sight,
Or swiftly driven from our Coast.

The Foe comes on with haughty stride,
Our troops advance with martial noise.
Their Vet'rans flee before our Youth,
And Gen'rals yield to beardless Boys.

What grateful Off'ring shall we bring?
What shall we render to the Lord?
Loud Halleluiahs let us sing.
And praise His name on ev'ry Chord.

Jeremiah Ingalls' *Christian Harmony* of 1805 was a popular, eclectic collection. Here is his NORTHFIELD (PftL 403) from an 1848 publication. The melody is in the tenor line and would have been sung by tenors and some sopranos, while other sopranos sang the topmost line. The first five measures of the piece are straightforward and chordal. With the sixth measure, a series of successive entrances begins. Ingalls and others called works like this "fuging tunes," having borrowed the imitative entrances from earlier adventurous British models that were called "fuging psalm tunes." Ingalls is also the source of CHARITY (PftL 279).

American hymnody

Even though Watts' and Wesley's hymns gained popularity during the Great Awakening, no American poet would claim the hymnist's mantle for decades. Timothy Dwight's "I Love Thy Kingdom, Lord" (PftL 289, 290), a paraphrase of Psalm 137, is the earliest American hymn in common use. Dwight (1752-1817), a grandson of Jonathan Edwards and president of Yale College, was America's first important hymnist. He published a hymnal in 1800 which included works by many established hymnists along with some of his own. On the musical side, Oliver Holden's CORONATION (PftL 19), written in 1793, is the earliest American-composed tune still in common usage.

But the most significant innovations from this newly independent country were not to come from the well-educated Easterners. A movement was brewing in the western frontier that would redirect the course of hymnody in the United States and abroad.

The Great Revival and camp meeting songs

In August 1801, at the invitation of Barton W. Stone and other ministers, large numbers of settlers gathered around the Cane Ridge Meeting House in Bourbon County, Kentucky. Military observers estimated the crowd to consist of twenty thousand to thirty thousand people who had brought their tents and their camping equipment in order to stay for several days; to enjoy fellowship; to hear Presbyterian, Baptist, and Methodist ministers proclaim the gospel; and to dance, shout, and sing. This meeting was the largest of a number of similar events that began around 1800 and constituted the most visible aspect of the movement that came to be known variously as The Second Great Awakening or as The Great Revival. Touched by the power of the Spirit and reinvigorated, participants returned to their cabins and settlements to join small but growing churches.

This meeting, his growing disaffection with creedal separatism, his association with ministers of other denominations, and his desire for non-denominational Christianity led Stone, along with five other Presbyterian ministers, to sign the "Last Will and Testament of the Springfield Presbytery" on June 28, 1804, in the Cane Ridge Meeting House. Twenty years later he was to collaborate with Alexander Campbell in the development of a Restoration Movement that was to lead toward the establishment of the Church of Christ and the Disciples of Christ.

Those who participated in this revival and similar events were largely illiterate and without common church music traditions. But they enjoyed folk music and dance music, and they participated enthusiastically in promoting a new genre of church song, which came to be known as camp-meeting songs or frontier songs. These were simple, catchy, repetitive, largely improvised, and easily learned. They were as much social as spiritual, and they could be carried back home and shared with neighbors.

As one might suppose, the appeal of these songs would not be limited to the frontier. They migrated eastward and were enthusiastically received and published during the first half of the nineteenth century in collections such as *The evangelical harp: a new collection of hymns and tunes, designed for revivals of religion, and for family and social worship / by Jacob Knapp. Containing also, an essay on evangelism / by the compiler* (Utica, New York, 1845); *Zion's Harp or a New Collection of Music intended as a companion to Village Hymns for Social Worship*, published by Rev. Asahel Nettleton (New Haven, N. & S.S. Jocelyn, 1824); and Joshua Leavitt's *The Christian Lyre* (1831). These publications contained a variety of church music, including both traditional hymns and the more robust new material. "The Last Trumpet" from *The evangelical harp* illustrates the jaunty simplicity of tunes that could serve equally well for preaching at the mourner's bench or for fiddling and dancing at the family wagon after the meeting.

2. *He'll encompass land and ocean, ocean, ocean, Encompass land and ocean at the end of time.*
3. *You will see the graves a bursting, &c.*
4. *You will see this world on fire, &c.*
5. *There will be an awful shaking, &c.*
6. *How will you stand it sinner, &c.*
7. *You will wish you were forgiven, &c.*
8. *But saints will not be frightened, &c.*
9. *They'll rise and meet their Jesus, &c.*
10. *He will lead them to his kingdom, &c.*
11. *Then the warfare will be ended, &c.*
12. *We will shout above the fire, &c.*

Meanwhile, some Southerners were singing texts by Watts and Wesley and others to simple tunes of uncertain, folk-inspired provenance. These tunes often used only five notes of the scale and are thus called pentatonic. The most familiar of these tunes is NEW BRITAIN, shown here as it appeared in *Southern Harmony* (published by William Walker, 1835) with Newton's text from fifty-six years earlier.

Many of these pentatonic tunes, such as BALLERMA (PftL 465), BEACH SPRING (PftL 915), CHARITY (PftL 279), CLEANSING FOUNTAIN (PftL 662), FOUNDATION (PftL 248), and HOLY MANNA (PftL 974), survive in modern hymnals.

The Sacred Harp

Interest in shape notes, musical instruction, and singing schools waned in the Northeast around 1815. In the South, however, there was still an enthusiastic market for singing practice, and collections such as Walker's *Southern Harmony* were widely used for this purpose.

Benjamin Franklin White (1800-79) led singing schools throughout west Georgia. In 1844 he and E. J. King,[3] one of his students, published *The Sacred Harp*, which consisted of more than 250 songs that the two had written, compiled, or arranged. The eclectic contents included traditional psalms and hymns, fuging tunes, pentatonic folk hymns, and camp-meeting songs, printed with shape notes in three or four voice parts.

In order to promote the new hymnal, White organized and conducted special singing events, the first of which was the Southern Musical Convention, established in Huntersville, Georgia, in 1845, with the purpose of

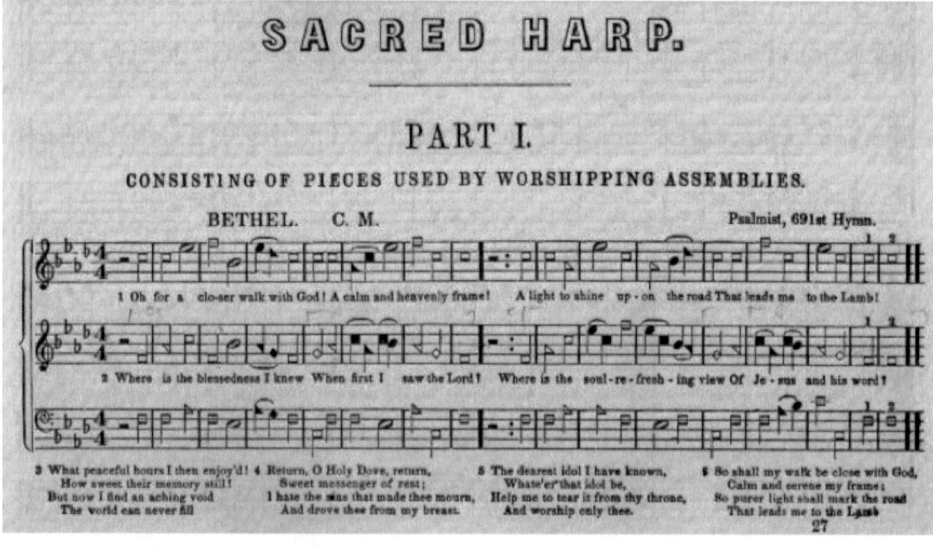

---

[3] Unfortunately, King died shortly before the initial press run of 1,500 books arrived in Georgia from the Philadelphia printer.

meeting regularly to learn church music. *The Sacred Harp* was the convention's textbook. These singing conventions combined social gatherings, revivals, pot-luck meals, music instruction, performance, and worship, and they were widely imitated and long-lived.

The Chattahoochee Sacred Harp Convention of Carrollton, Georgia, was organized in 1852 and continues to the present, having met yearly with only a few lapses. The East Texas Sacred Harp Convention has met in several counties since 1855 and now gathers regularly in Henderson, Texas. Similar gatherings occur in different parts of the country.

The Sacred Harp went through three revisions, all under the auspices of the Southern Musical Convention. Here is the opening song from the second edition, which contained the original contents and added an appendix of new songs.

Lowell Mason

Shape notes flourished in the South; Lowell Mason (1792-1872) campaigned against them in the East. Wishing to establish a higher quality of church music than that represented by the folksy camp meeting songs, he compiled a hymnal for the Boston Handel and Haydn Society in 1822 and published eight of his own collections, beginning with *Spiritual Songs for Social Worship* in 1832. His opposition to shape notes and to tunes that he considered crude was a part of his "better music" movement. In order to improve music reading and congregational singing, he campaigned for general music instruction and led the movement that established music as a part of the Boston public school curriculum in 1838.

Mason was more than a musical activist. He was a talented composer with a keen sense for good hymn tunes. He wrote more than 1200 of them, many of which are still used today. Among these are BOYLSTON ("A Charge to Keep I Have," PftL 3 and 258), ERNAN ("Go, Labor On." PftL 176), GERAR ("God Is the Fountain Whence," PftL 184), BEALOTH ("I Love Thy Kingdom, Lord," PftL 290), ANTIOCH ("Joy to the World," PftL 376), OLIVET ("My Faith Looks Up to Thee," PftL 442), BETHANY ("Nearer, My God, to Thee," PftL 450), PEREZ ("Praise the Lord," PftL 531), ZERAH ("To Us a Child of Hope Is Born," PftL 710), HAMBURG ("When I Survey the Wondrous Cross," PftL 742, based loosely on a Gregorian recitation formula), and scores of others that are still familiar.

Organs, choirs, Campbellites, Shakers, and Mormons

Some church leaders chose other means for improving singing and installed organs to accompany congregational song. An early publication supporting their use had an enlightening title: *The lawfulness, excellency and advantages of instrumental music in the worship of God urg'd and enforc'd from scripture and the examples of the far greater part of Christians of all ages. Addressed to all (particularly the Presbyterians and Baptists) who have hitherto been taught to look upon the use of instrumental musick in the worship of God as unlawful. By a Presbyterian. Philadelphia, 1763.* As might be inferred, most American churches maintained a non-instrumental stance, but some more affluent congregations, particularly in the North and on the East Coast, began to use organs in order to raise their relative status and improve the musical experience in their services. Through the nineteenth century, particularly after the Civil War, organs were adopted in ever-increasing numbers by congregations that had formerly opposed their usage. The issue was a divisive one.

In some congregations, groups of interested singers acquired special training through singing schools and special musical instruction, sat together during services, and sang strongly in an attempt to lead others to a more rewarding musical performance. They might occasionally present a hymn during the service, and the number of organized choirs in American churches increased. In some congregations choirs largely supplanted congregational singing, and as the influence of the Oxford Movement (see chapter 10) worked through the United States these church choirs might be robed and participate in processionals.

There was also a counter movement towards improving congregational singing. Henry Ward Beecher, the minister of the Congregational Plymouth Church in Brooklyn Heights, New York, was interested in developing a singing church. In order to do away with the practice of lining out hymns and to bring the music to the congregation, he compiled and published *The Plymouth Collection of Hymns and Tunes* (1855, with 1,374 hymns), with words and music on the same page, and put copies in the hands of those who sat in the pews. The influence of Beecher and his hymnal spread widely, and hymnals were used congregationally in many denominations. Some hymnals were produced independently, some with the official sanction of a denominational governing board.

Singing played an important role in three groups that developed in nineteenth-century America. Alexander Campbell (1788-1866), an Irish immigrant, was a co-founder of a religious movement, established Bethany College, wrote several books, published journals, and produced a hymnal with a distinctly scriptural name. His *Psalms, Hymns, and Spiritual Songs*, published in 1828 in Bethany, Virginia,[4] contained no tunes, because he was opposed to musical notation in hymnals, to singing schools, and to any device that might tend to make music more than a mere vehicle for the text. A fine administrator and preacher, Campbell was not as talented as a poet. His texts are stiff and pedantic, and hymnal editors have found them easy to overlook. He contributed a few texts to his hymnal, including "Upon the Banks of Jordan Stood" (PftL 692, with an un-Campbell-like refrain). His followers and those of Barton W. Stone joined forces in an attempt to reject denominationalism and "restore New Testament Christianity." Often labeled "Campbellites," they, along with many Mennonites, have maintained a sturdy non-instrumental tradition.

Ann Lee and her followers emigrated from England in 1774; they came to be known as the Shaking Quakers, or the Shakers. Their communities flourished for a time and were known for their industry, their creativity, their celibacy (which was to lead to their demise, after they were denied the privilege of replenishing their numbers from orphanages), and their music. The best known of their songs, "Simple Gifts," refers to their religious dancing in its refrain: "When true simplicity is gained, to bow and to bend we shan't be ashamed; to turn, turn will be our delight, till by turning, turning we come round right."

The Church of Jesus Christ of Latter-Day Saints originated and developed under the leadership of Joseph Smith in the 1820s and, after his death in 1844, Brigham Young. Hymnody has been central to their religious culture, and the Mormon Tabernacle Choir is known throughout the country. The song "Come, Come, Ye Saints" (PftL 106), written in 1846 by William Clayton and sung to a Sacred Harp tune, was an important anthem on the group's westward migration and still holds a place of honor in the church's repertoire.

---

[4] Bethany is in the part of the state that broke away in 1863 and is now West Virginia.

CHAPTER 10

DEVELOPMENTS IN BRITISH HYMNODY

Large Anglican churches in Britain usually enjoyed music provided by trained performers. Singing in the independent Methodist, Baptist, and Congregationalist churches or in small Anglican churches was less impressive, and there were attempts to improve its quality. On occasion, volunteer groups of singers (mostly male) practiced the songs that were to be sung, learning them in three or four parts, and essentially became an informal church choir, usually sitting together in the west gallery of the auditoriums. By the middle of the eighteenth century organs, and even church bands, were used in a number of British churches in order to support the singing of choirs and congregations. Thomas Webster's "The Village Choir" (1847) depicts a Christmas morning service in a rural church in England in 1820, with informal musical assistance from the west gallery.

The Village Choir (ca. 1847) - Thomas Webster

The tradition of the West Gallery Singers[1] became well established in England.

An authorized hymnal

The most outstanding hymnist of the early nineteenth century in England was James Montgomery (1771-1854), the author of "Angels from the Realms of Glory" (PftL 42), "Hail to the Lord's Anointed" (PftL 201), and "In the Hour of Trial" (PftL 328). He was a close friend of Thomas Cotterill (1779-1823) of Sheffield, and the two collaborated to produce *A Selection of Psalms and Hymns for Public and Private Use, Adapted to the Services of the Church of England*, which Cotterill published. The collection contained 150 psalms and 367 hymns, many of them by Montgomery and Cotterill, though authorship was not attributed in the book. The book was extremely popular and came to be used by some Anglican congregations. It was in its ninth printing by 1820, when Cotterill was brought into court to face the charge of unauthorized publication of a church hymnal.

The matter was settled when the Archbishop of York became involved. He issued his own version of the collection, with fewer hymns and an organization parallel to that of *The Book of Common Prayer*. With his authorization, the hymnal began to be used in Anglican services in Yorkshire. Although Cotterill's collection had earlier been suppressed, the revised collaborative version became familiar to an increasing number of churchgoing Anglicans.

In England, as in America, many nineteenth-century publications included, along with hymns, instructions on how to sing them. Joseph Mainzer (1801-51) and John Hullah (1812-84) were two leaders in the musical revival and "singing class" movement.

While Methodist and evangelical groups continued to enjoy their less sophisticated songs, among some Anglicans there was an increased interest in the quality of both music and poetry. William Gardiner (1770-1853), of Leicester, published *Sacred Melodies, From Haydn, Mozart and*

---

[1] Early Christian tradition called for the altar to be placed on the east side of the church building. Some Protestant groups followed this convention, placing the pulpit to the east; so the west gallery would be the balcony at the back of the auditorium, facing the speaker. This West Gallery Singers were similar to the informal groups that supported American congregational singing as described at the end of the previous chapter.

Beethoven. Adapted to the best English Poets, and Appropriated to the use of the British Church in 1815 (PftL 467, 501, 794), and others followed his lead in adapting melodies from the masters for hymn tunes.

The hymn texts of Thomas Kelly (1769-1855, author of "The Head That Once Was Crowned with Thorns," PftL 639) and Reginald Heber (1783-1826) illustrate a new literary emphasis. Inspired by the *Olney Hymns*, Heber began writing for his own congregation, according to the requirements of the church year. In 1823 he was appointed to be the Bishop of Calcutta, where he spent the last three years of his life in dedicated service. Some of his texts are still commonly used, most notably "Holy, Holy, Holy" (PftL 238). J. B. Dykes' NICAEA, invariably paired with the text today, was not composed until 1861. Its title references the Nicene Creed, which codified the doctrine of the Trinity in A.D. 325. Ironically, this doctrine has been written out of the hymn in some hymnals, including *Praise for the Lord*.[2] Here are Heber's original words, with their Trinitarian proclamation.

Holy, holy, holy! Lord God Almighty!
Early in the morning our song shall rise to thee;
holy, holy, holy! merciful and mighty,
God in three persons, blessed Trinity!

Holy, holy, holy! All the saints adore thee,
casting down their golden crowns around the glassy sea;
cherubim and seraphim falling down before thee,
who wert and art and evermore shalt be.

Holy, holy, holy! Though the darkness hide thee,
though the eye made blind by sin thy glory may not see,
only thou art holy; there is none beside thee,
perfect in power, in love, and purity.

Holy, holy, holy! Lord God Almighty!
All thy works shall praise thy name, in earth and sky and sea;
holy, holy, holy! merciful and mighty,
God in three persons, blessed Trinity!

---

[2] The last line of the first and last stanzas in the altered version reads, "God over all, and blest eternally."

The Oxford Movement

John Keble, an ordained priest and former tutor at Oxford University, published in 1827 *The Christian Year*, a book of poems for meditation on Sundays and feast days throughout the church year. This collection (which included the poem "Sun of My Soul, Thou Savior Dear," PftL 593) was well received and widely distributed, and he was appointed to the Chair of Poetry at Oxford. Alarmed by the success of the Methodists and Evangelicals, in 1833 he preached his famous "National Apostasy" sermon, calling for a return to and reform of the established church. Thus began the "Tractarian" or "Oxford Movement," which brought greater emphasis to the functions of the clergy, the sacraments, and the liturgy. Another leader of the movement, John Henry Newman (PftL 385), was so convicted by the call for a return to the church's roots that he later arranged an audience with the Pope, converted, and became a Cardinal in the Catholic Church. As the movement's tenets took hold, Anglican music was purged of secularisms and common poetry, and renewed attention was given to ancient tunes and texts. Hundreds of translations of Greek, Latin, and German texts appeared, and plainchants were adapted for congregational or choral use. John Mason Neale (1818-66, PftL 43, 47, 81, 489, 625) and Catherine Winkworth (1827-78, PftL 109, 324, 361, 457, 458, 534) were important translators.

The most significant hymnal to appear as a result of the Oxford Movement was *Hymns Ancient and Modern* (1861). Arranged according to *The Book of Common Prayer*, it contained many translated hymns and served as the model for later hymnals. It "married" a number of particular texts and tunes in partnerships that have been preserved in English hymnody, and the hymnal remained immensely popular through several editions.

Without question, the predominant composer of the Oxford Movement was John Bacchus Dykes (1823-76), who wrote more than 300 tunes, many of which first appeared in *Hymns Ancient and Modern* and are well known today in American and British churches. Besides NICAEA, these include BEATITUDO ("O for a Closer Walk With God," PftL 461), LUX BENIGNA ("Lead, Kindly Light," PftL 385), MELITA ("Eternal Father, Strong to Save," PftL 128), ST. AGNES ("Jesus, the Very Thought of Thee," PftL 373), and ST. SYLVESTER ("Father, Hear the Prayer We Offer," PftL 144). During Victorian times, many hymn settings became more harmonically sophisticated and more musically demanding.

The Oxford Movement had lasting effects on British hymnody, producing a desire to maintain a high quality of words and music along with an awareness of the history and development of hymnody. Robert Bridges' *Yattendon Hymnal* (1899) illustrated the literary emphasis of its editor, the Poet Laureate of England. Certifying the flourishing academic interest in the subject, John Julian's *Dictionary of Hymnology* was first published in 1892, a magnificent work signaling and encouraging an interest in hymnology. The Hymn Society of America was established in 1922, and writers such as Louis F. Benson and Erik Routley have contributed significantly to the field.

Rugby School, in Warwickshire, published *Psalms and Hymns for the Use of Rugby School Chapel* before 1837, and other British public schools (private schools for boys) followed this lead, producing proprietary hymnals, emphasizing unison singing with organ accompaniment, with texts and music of high quality. We must pay particular attention to the hymn "Jerusalem" (next page), created by the marriage of a poem by William Blake (1804, "And Did Those Feet in Ancient Time") to a tune by Sir Hubert Parry from 1916. It is, unofficially, England's national hymn, and it is sung regularly in schools and churches, annually at the last night of the Proms in Royal Albert Hall, and before sporting events. The film *Chariots of Fire* (1981) took its title from a line in the hymn.

An American edition of *Hymns Ancient and Modern* appeared in 1862, and it was a model for succeeding Episcopalian and Presbyterian hymnals. American evangelical churches were little affected by the Oxford Movement.

The Welsh are known for their singing and for contributing a number of hymn tunes to the common repertoire. Two favorites are EBENEZER (PftL 198), composed by Thomas John Williams (1869-1944) and first published around 1900; and CWM RHONDDA (PftL 187), by John Hughes (1873-1932), written for a singing festival in 1903.

During the latter part of the nineteenth century, Scottish Presbyterians forsook exclusive psalmody and took up hymn singing.

Jerusalem

William Blake

Charles H. H. Parry

And did those feet in an- cient_ time Walk up-on Eng-land's moun-tains green? And was the Ho - ly Lamb of__ God On Eng-land's plea-sant pas-tures seen? And did the coun - te-nance di- vine Shine forth up - on our cloud-ed hills? And was Je ru-sa-lem build-ed here A-mong these dark sa-ta-nic mills?

Twentieth-century hymnals

Three influential British hymnals were produced in the early part of the century. In 1906 Percy Dearmer published *The English Hymnal*, with Ralph Vaughan Williams (1872-1958) as musical editor. Dearmer was interested in exploring and reestablishing medieval British traditions, and Vaughan Williams used some old English folk tunes in the collection, including KINGSFOLD, a tune which probably originated before the sixteenth century. It might have been used by Sternhold for his psalm settings 460 years earlier; if so, Dearmer and Vaughan Williams returned to it a churchly connection, pairing it with Horatio Bonar's "I Heard the Voice of Jesus Say." It is also used with Louis Benson's "O Sing a Song of Bethlehem" and is associated with the Irish folk song "The Star of County Down."

Vaughan Williams,who would become one of the most significant British composers of his time, wrote his SINE NOMINE (PftL 155) for this hymnal. He and Dearmer later collaborated with Martin Shaw to produce *Songs of Praise* (1925) and the *Oxford Book of Carols* (1928).

Religious fervor declined in England after World War I, along with church attendance and hymn singing. As religion became more of a social and cultural commitment, hymn texts have become less doctrinal, less scripturally based, and more expressive of social responsibility, cultural diversity, and environmental awareness. Many hymnal committees have taken pains to purge songs of sexist and archaic terminology. Hymn music has been influenced by popular styles, by chants, by spirituals, and by the introduction of tunes from other cultures. Among the leading British poets of recent hymns are Fred Pratt Green (1903-2000), author of "For the Fruit of All Creation" (PftL 919), "O Christ, the Healer" (PftL 957), and "When Jesus Came to Jordan" (PftL 981); Fred Kaan (1929-2009); and Brian Wren (b. 1936), author of "Christ Is Alive!" (PftL 98), "I Come with Joy" (PftL 913), and "Jesus, On the Mountain Peak" (PftL 930).

O Sing a Song of Bethlehem

Louis Benson

KINGSFOLD

CHAPTER 11

GOSPEL AND CONVENTION SONGS

A merican antebellum churches were often split between northern and southern groups — among the chief dividing issues were slavery, church government and authority, instrumental music, and musical styles. In general, southern churches were less affluent, less well educated, less sophisticated; and more likely to reject instruments and abolitionism.

Around 1857, a new wave of religious fervor swept the Northeast, powered by political uncertainty and a financial panic. Along with this Great Awakening of 1857 came interdenominational noonday prayer meetings, a renewed interest in evangelism and philanthropy, and the establishment of Sunday Schools.[1]

The Young Men's Christian Association had been established in London in 1844 by George Williams as a ministry to young men drawn to the cities by the Industrial Revolution. During the 1860s the YMCA made inexpensive and safe housing available for young men in American cities. Chicago's Farwell Hall, the first American YMCA dormitory, was completed in 1867. This development both represented and drove the religious renewal.

Gospel songs

William Bradbury (1816-68), who had studied in Boston under Lowell Mason and who shared Mason's passion for musical education, moved to Brooklyn, taught free singing schools that were popularly attended, and started the Bradbury Piano Company. He observed that the songs that were most favored in this revivalist era were not Mason's sedate hymns, but

---

[1] Sunday schools had been introduced in Methodist churches after the Revolutionary War, often teaching reading and writing as well as Bible topics.

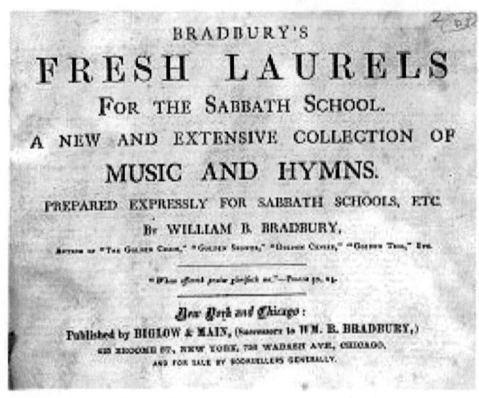

songs that reflected influences from folk songs, camp meeting songs, and modern parlor songs.[2] He wrote a number of pieces exhibiting these qualities for his Sunday School collections, such as "He Leadeth Me" (PftL 216), "Jesus Loves Me" (1862, PftL 810), "Just As I Am" (PftL 380), "My Hope Is Built on Nothing Less" (PftL 438), and "Sweet Hour of Prayer" (PftL 618).

It became obvious that the songs' appeal was not limited to the young, and other composers fell in line to satisfy the changing demand.

Songs and evangelism

Philip P. Bliss (1838-76), a talented musician with little formal training, met Bradbury in 1857 and became an itinerant music teacher. In 1864 he moved to Chicago, where he established himself as a teacher, singer, and composer of church songs. In 1869 the evangelist Dwight L. Moody (1837-99) urged him to become a full-time missionary singer, and in 1874 Bliss began singing in the evangelistic campaigns of Major D. W. Whittle. In the same year he published a small collection entitled *Gospel Songs for Gospel Meetings*, and in 1875 he and Ira D. Sankey produced *Gospel Hymns and Sacred Songs*.

The term "Gospel Song" came to be associated with works that often included refrains after each stanza; simple and predictable harmonies, often with only three or four chords in a song; a bit of jaunty rhythmic interest; and simple, straightforward, and encouraging texts. Bradbury, Bliss, and Sankey provided a foundation upon which scores of writers would build for over a century.

Bliss and his wife died in a train wreck in 1876, but his legacy still rings loudly in American churches, with songs such as "Almost Persuaded" (PftL 31), "Hallelujah! What a Savior!" (PftL 203), "Let the Lower Lights Be Burning" (PftL 397), "More Holiness Give Me" (PftL 434), and "Wonderful Words of Life" (PftL 788); and tunes such as CLEARFIELD

---

[2] The songs of Stephen Foster (1826-64) were popular throughout the country.

("I Bring My Sins to Thee," PftL 262), KENOSIS ("I Gave My Life for Thee," PftL 268). and VILLE DU HAVRE ("It Is Well with My Soul," written for a poem by Horatio Spafford, another associate of Moody, PftL 345).

After Bliss's death, Major Whittle employed James McGranahan (1840-1907) as his musical collaborator. McGranahan produced the tunes for a number of texts by Whittle and others; it was McGranahan who provided the familiar gospel song setting for Neumeister's "Sinners Jesus Will Receive" (PftL 588).

Ira D. Sankey (1840-1908), song leader, writer, and soloist, began working with Dwight Moody in 1870. The two were conducting a gospel meeting in Chicago in 1871 when the great fire broke out. In 1872 they made the first of a number of trips to England to conduct evangelistic services. Sankey carried a small portable organ, a harmonium, on his tours, accompanying himself while he sang. It was during one of these meetings in 1874 that Sankey improvised a tune to Elizabeth Clephane's poem, creating the familiar song "The Ninety and Nine" (PftL 651). His British campaigns hclpcd to popularize gospel songs in that country.

After collaborating with P.P. Bliss in *Gospel Hymns and Sacred Songs*, Sankey worked with James McGranahan and George C. Stebbins to produce church songs which the Moody Bible Institute (founded in Chicago in 1890) helped to distribute and popularize. His tunes include "Faith Is the Victory" (PftL 134), "For You I Am Praying" (PftL 270), "Shelter in the Time of Storm" (PftL 575), "Simply Trusting" (PftL 582), "Still, Still with Thee" (PftL 597), and "Under His Wings" (PftL 715). His tunes often have no names other than the first words of the texts with which they were published. With gospel songs, there are no more interchangeable tunes; words and music are locked together.

After Moody and Sankey, Charles ("Charlie") Alexander (1867-1920) and Homer Rodeheaver (1880-1955) became prominent church music leaders. Alexander, traveling with evangelist Reuben Torrey in Australia, began to use Robert Harkness as his piano accompanist. Harkness tired of the harmonic monotony of the gospel songs and, with Alexander's encouragement, introduced new piano stylings. He went on to publish *The Harkness Piano Method of Evangelistic Hymn Playing* (1941) and set the style for gospel pianists to follow. Alexander and Harkness popularized

"The Glory Song" ("When All My Labors and Trials," PftL 169), which was amenable to many musical effects.

Rodeheaver was the song leader for the evangelist Billy Sunday and was famous for his clever banter and his vocal and trombone solos. Criticized for a secular-sounding hymn,[3] he responded, "It was never intended for a Sunday morning service, not for a devotional meeting — its purpose was to bridge the gap between the popular song of the day and the great hymns and gospel songs, and to give men a simple, easy lilting melody which they could learn the first time they heard it, and which they could whistle and sing wherever they might be."

We have read earlier of Augustine's and Wesley's reservations about the seductive quality of music. Rodeheaver's statement is the first clear expression we have encountered of an intent to use this quality as an attraction to draw newcomers to an encounter with the gospel message. It was with Alexander's and Rodeheaver's generation that music became a deliberate lure to the unchurched, a role that it would continue to serve in many fellowships.

In England, as in America, a spirit of evangelical revival spread in the mid- and late-nineteenth century. The gospel songs introduced by Moody and Sankey found fertile soil in independent churches. American and British missionaries have aided in their dispersal, and gospel songs are now sung in many languages throughout the world.

Other gospel song writers

Ira Sankey was blind for the last five years of his life and found comfort in his friendship and collaboration with Fanny Crosby (1820-1915). Born to poor parents in eastern New York state, Crosby had been blinded at the age of six weeks by inept medical treatment. When she was a year old her father died, and she was raised with a strong religious grounding by her mother and grandmother; at fifteen she was enrolled in the New York Institute for the Blind.

---

[3] The song was "Brighten the Corner Where You Are," written by Charles Gabriel and copyrighted and published by The Rodeheaver Company, introducing a commercial element to the performances.

She showed talent as a poet from youth, and when she was eight she wrote

Oh what a happy soul I am,
Although I cannot see;
I am resolved that in this world
Contented I will be.
How many blessings I enjoy,
That other people don't;
To weep and sigh because I'm blind,
I cannot, and I won't.

But she didn't begin producing the works by which she is now known until 1863, when, at the urging of William Bradbury, she produced her first hymn text. She would ultimately produce more than eight thousand texts that would be sung to music written by Bradbury, Sankey, Bliss, Phillip Phillips, Phoebe Palmer Knapp, and many others. Her chief musical collaborator was William H. Doane (1832-1915). Scores of her songs appear in hymnals today, including "All the Way My Savior Leads Me" (PftL 22), "Blessed Assurance" (PftL 71), "Close to Thee" (PftL 101), "I Am Thine, O Lord" (PftL 261), "Jesus Is Tenderly Calling Thee Home" (PftL 356), "Nearer the Cross" (PftL 439), "Pass Me Not, O Gentle Savior" (PftL 526), "Praise Him, Praise Him" (PftL 532), "Rescue the Perishing" (PftL 551), "Safe in the Arms of Jesus" (PftL 559), and "To God Be the Glory" (PftL 682).

Robert Lowry (1826-99) was an occasional collaborator with Fanny Crosby, a professor of literature at the University of Lewisburg (now Bucknell), a Baptist minister, and a musical editor for the Biglow Publishing Company. But he is perhaps best remembered for two songs which he both authored and composed — "Shall We Gather at the River" (PftL 570) and "How Can I Keep from Singing"—and for providing a popular musical setting for Watts' hymn "Come We That Love the Lord" (PftL 111).

Another important composer was William J. Kirkpatrick (1838-1921), who wrote HE HIDETH MY SOUL (PftL 9), LEAD ME TO CALVARY (PftL 384), LORD I'M COMING HOME (PftL 414), O TO BE LIKE THEE (PftL 499), REDEEMED (PftL 544), 'TIS SO SWEET TO TRUST IN JESUS (PftL 687), and hundreds of other tunes; and published about 50 hymn collections.

The gospel song has been a popular genre. In denominations with publishing committees that officially produce and sanction hymnals, gospel songs are represented in limited numbers. But among denominations with hymnals that are essentially commercial ventures, especially in the South, they are prominent.

Convention songs

Singing conventions continued to be popular in the South, and many adopted gospel songs into their repertoires. But there was new musical territory to be explored — and exploited. The popularity of Alexander and Rodeheaver had demonstrated that church music could not only be appealing to a wide audience but also marketable. James D. Vaughan (1864-1941) founded the James D. Vaughan Publishing Company in 1900, and in 1910 he sent a professional quartet on the road for the purpose of selling his songbooks. He founded a radio station in 1922 and broadcast Southern gospel music; and his Vaughan Phonograph Records was the first recording company in the South.

Virgil O. Stamps (1892-1940) worked with Vaughan's publishing company and sang in Vaughan's quartet. In 1915 he wrote his first song, and in 1924 he established the V.O. Stamps Music Company and the V.O. Stamps School of Music. In 1927 he founded, with J.R. Baxter, the Stamps-Baxter Publishing Company in Dallas. His Stamps Quartet was given a daily broadcast on the Dallas radio station KRLD in 1936.

The songs published by these companies are called "convention songs," "quartet songs," "white gospel," or, because of their close association with the publishing company, "Stamps-Baxter songs." Rooted in the style of the gospel song, they add new features, such as solo vocal leads, moderate chromaticism, and significant rhythmic interest, including syncopation. Stamps-Baxter songs in PftL include "He Bore It All" (820), "I Love My Savior, Too" (825), "Salvation Has Been Brought Down" (834), "Sing Me a Song About Jesus" (835), "The New Song" (837), "When All of God's Singers Get Home" (839), "Sing and Be Happy" (841) — and many others.

Although they were often introduced by professional quartets, the convention songs were adopted, as was the publishers' intent, for congregational use. The new musical styles were attractive to some but considered inappropriate by others, and congregations were sometimes split by musical tastes. Over time, convention songs lost their association with performing groups and were written directly for congregational use, as in "Our God, He Is Alive," by A. W. Dicus (1966, PftL 523).

Gospel singing conventions, combining congregational singing and vocal quartets or other small ensembles, were common into the 1940s. Their popularity declined somewhat after World War II as radio, television, and affluence introduced competing forms of entertainment. But they continue in some parts of the South, and a Stamps-Baxter School of Music meets every summer.

Chapter 12

CONTINUITY AND CHANGE

Religion retained an important place in the lives and culture of Americans well into the twentieth century, and church attendance was customary. By the early 1900s most congregations were using organs or pianos, the latter being less expensive, easier to play, and more amenable to various genres of music.

John Greenleaf Whittier was a harbinger of an American movement paralleling the British trend toward social and gender awareness and relaxed dogmatic conviction. This universalist and abolitionist poem of 1850 by Whittier, proclaiming the necessity of social responsibility, found a place in many hymnals.

O brother man, fold to thy heart thy brother;
Where pity dwells, the peace of God is there;
To worship rightly is to love each other,
Each smile a hymn, each kindly deed a prayer.

For he whom Jesus loved has truly spoken:
The holier worship which He deigns to bless
Restores the lost, and binds the spirit broken,
And feeds the widow and the fatherless.

Follow with reverent steps the great example
Of Him Whose holy work was doing good;
So shall the wide earth seem our Father's temple,
Each loving life a psalm of gratitude.

Then shall all shackles fall; the stormy clangor
Of wild war music o'er the earth shall cease;
Love shall tread out the baleful fire of anger,
And in its ashes plant the tree of peace.

Two editions of *The Methodist Hymnal* (1936, 1966) have been among the most influential hymnals of the century. Harry Emerson Fosdick's marvelously alliterative "God of Grace and God of Glory" (1930, PftL 187) was introduced in the first of these.

Though outside of the mainstream of American hymnody, Lloyd O. Sanderson (1901-92) has had some influence in Churches of Christ, as writer, composer, and publisher. One of his collaborators (on songs such as "Be With Me, Lord" [PftL 40], "Bring Christ Your Broken Life," and "Buried With Christ" [PftL 85]) was Thomas Chisholm (1866-1960), who also authored "Great Is Thy Faithfulness" (1923, with William Runyan, PftL 190), "Living for Jesus" (1917, with C. Harold Lowden, PftL 402), "O to Be Like Thee" (1897, with William Kirkpatrick, PftL 499), and "Only in Thee" (1905, with Charles Gabriel, PftL 519).

Gospel music and spirituals

Predominately Black churches developed understandably different traditions, often incorporating elements of blues, jazz, and distinctive piano stylings. Other instruments have been added over the years. Thomas A. Dorsey (1899-1993),[1] who began his career as a blues pianist, is often known as "the father of Black gospel music." In 1932, mourning the death of his wife and infant son, he adapted a tune written in 1844 by George Allen (PftL 427) and produced "Precious Lord, Take My Hand" (PftL 610). In 1937 he wrote "Peace in the Valley" for the singer Mahalia Jackson. After she recorded it, the song was covered by Johnny Cash, Red Foley, Connie Francis, George Jones, Little Richard, Loretta Lynn, Ronnie Milsap, and Elvis Presley. Red Foley's version was the first gospel song to sell over a million copies.

The path of the Black spiritual is largely separate from congregational song until the second half of the twentieth century. Early sources such as *Slave Songs of the United States*[2] contain a variety of short calls and refrains, but not "Swing Low, Sweet Chariot," "Wade in the Water," "Deep River," or other songs currently considered classics of the repertoire. The

[1] Born in Villa Rica, Georgia, Dorsey moved to Chicago in 1916 and studied at the Chicago School of Composition and Arranging. As a blues player, he was known as "Georgia Tom." In the early 1930s he began working with choirs in three Chicago churches.

[2] by William Francis Allen, Charles Pickard Ware, and Lucy McKim Garrison, New York, A. Simpson & Co., 1867.

first significant presentation of spirituals outside of the black community came with the tours of the Fisk Jubilee Singers, beginning in 1871. Their manager and director, George L. White, a Caucasian, made "proper" arrangements of tunes which he heard the group singing informally. After their performance at the Plymouth Church in Brooklyn and their endorsement by the church's pastor, Henry Ward Beecher, the fame of the Singers spread. They sang "Steal Away to Jesus" and "Go Down, Moses" in England for Queen Victoria in April of 1873 as they were touring Europe..

A similar group, the Hampton Singers of Hampton Institute in Virginia were established in 1870, two years before Booker T. Washington would enroll in that school.

Succeeding generations of composers[3] continued to develop, adapt, and arrange spirituals based on the traditions of the original folk idiom, and a recognizable repertoire emerged during the course of the twentieth century, ultimately finding its way into congregational song as Black churches embraced their own cultural heritage and as a sense of cultural inclusivity expanded the traditional repertoire of hymnals used in white congregations.

Commercialism and Christian music

By the early 1900s, Homer Rodeheaver, James D. Vaughan, and Virgil O. Stamps had effectively intermingled performance, publishing, and praise, and religious concert music was broadcast on the radio, made available in recordings, and published for personal and congregational use. Later, new styles of Christian music attracted audiences. Bill Gaither (b. 1936) began his career with the Bill Gaither Trio in the 1950s and went on to become an influential publisher, producer, and composer. Congregations have embraced his "Because He Lives" (PftL 68), "Something Beautiful" (PftL 885), and "There's Something About That Name" (PftL 889).

---

[3] John Wesley Work (c.1848-1923) directed a church choir in Nashville that included members of the original Jubilee Singers. His son John Wesley Work, Jr. (1871-1925), collected and arranged many spirituals and, like his son John Wesley Work III (1901-67), served as a director of the Jubilee Singers. R. Nathaniel Dett, the music director at Hampton 1913-32 went on to achieve significant attention as a performer and composer. The Fisk Jubilee Singers and the Hampton Singers continue to represent their respective institutions.

Other musicians, such as Mosie Lister ("He Knows Just What I Need," 1955, PftL 209; "How Long Has It Been?" 1956, PftL 251; "Let My Heart Be a Chapel," 1970, PftL 395; "Till the Storm Passes By," 1958, PftL 665; "Where No One Stands Alone," 1958, PftL 757), Doris Akers ("Sweet, Sweet Spirit," 1962, PftL 882), Twila Paris ("We Will Glorify," 1982, PftL 738; "We Bow Down," 1984, PftL 984; "Lamb of God," 1985, PftL 950) and Dennis Jernigan ("Thank You," 1992, PftL 975; "You Are My All in All," 1991, PftL 989), have followed Gaither's lead, mixing performance, composition, and publishing in styles that cross the bridge from the stage to the congregation.

The market for commercial Christian music in America has been strong, and many songs that were first heard in concert or broadcast made their way into congregational repertoire. This was not so true in England, where church attendance was lower and musical styles more traditional. In an effort to attract more youthful members, Geoffrey Beaumont (1904-71), chaplain at Trinity College, Cambridge, collaborated in the production in 1956 of the *20th Century Folk Mass*, with music that was more commonly associated with an English dance hall than a sanctuary. Two of his tunes were included in the 1962 *Baptist Hymn Book*.

Iconoclasts, worship wars, and the New Wave

America was rocked in the 1960s and '70s by protest, rebellion, and a deliberate rejection of tradition. The Calvary Chapel in Costa Mesa, California, was a center of new musical experimentation, eschewing traditional hymns in favor of songs influenced by pop music. Karen Lafferty's "Seek Ye First" (1971, PftL 883) became a hit at the chapel, spread through religious coffee houses and Jesus People connections, and eventually found a place in the standard congregational repertoire. Hundreds of works followed with characteristics including echo singing, vocal descants, texts that are often either scriptural or casually crafted, a folk-like style, and repetition. Young people of the 1970s embraced these new songs as their own new voice, typically rejecting traditional hymns.

As this new worship music spread, some older church members adapted to or adopted the newer repertoire, desiring to show camaraderie with and to encourage the continuing church attendance of the younger generation. Others, unwilling to give up their familiar songs or unable to appreciate the newer ones, refused to follow suit. During the years since the early

1970s members have migrated, and congregations have split. Some church leaders have designated different meeting times for those favoring older or newer forms, some have determined to use a "blended" approach, and many have learned to compromise in various ways.[4]

With the new repertoire came a return to the expectation of learning "by rote rather than by note." Since popular songs were passed along by word of mouth and by traveling performers and worship leaders, many favorites were not yet contained in a congregation's hymnal. Churches adapted by printing supplements or by projecting words on a screen or wall. It is difficult for printed hymnals to stay current in a fast-moving market.

Responding to criticisms that newer songs are often shallow and repetitive, some writers have produced thoughtfully crafted lyrics and sophisticated musical structures. Some, like "As the Deer" (Martin Nystrom, 1981, PftL 843) or "In Christ Alone" (Stuart Townend and Keith Getty, 2002), follow a more traditional strophic plan. Others remind us of seventeenth-century Pietism, which emphasized sentimentality, an awareness of personal guilt and the need for personal redemption, and an acute awareness of Christ's suffering on the behalf of each believer. A number of writers carefully craft textual and musical devices to elicit an emotional response, and trained worship leaders organize and choreograph the meeting's content in order to provide a validating "worship experience" for the congregation.

Congregations that sang with pianos or organs in the 1950s found that new musical styles require different instrumental forces. Guitars were often used during the 1960s; but many churches are now "plugged in," using electric guitars, keyboards, electric bass, drums, and, sometimes, wind instruments. The West Gallery Singers have been replaced by praise teams who sometimes sing with, sometimes perform for the assembly.

---

[4] For an interesting and debatable analysis of how the Baby Boomers changed worship styles through their numerical and financial clout and partially because of their rejection of tradition and cultural values, see Michael Hamilton's "A Generation Changes North American Hymnody."

Worship renewal

Among the churches adopting new musical styles is the Willow Creek Community Church, begun in 1975 near Chicago by founder and senior pastor Bill Hybels. Willow Creek has been a model in many ways, including evangelism, congregational organization, and music. The church's worship team develops a continuous thread of music to transition between songs and to underscore prayers, readings, and announcements.

Willow Creek helped to initiate an interest in worship renewal that transcended denominational boundaries, and many evangelical leaders searched for resources to bring similar experiences to their congregations. Worship ministry and worship renewal became recognized as a field of study, and Robert Webber's[5] Institute for Worship Studies established a doctoral-level program for potential worship ministers in 1999; a master's level program was added in 2002.

There is no common direction in Christian congregational music in recent years, there is considerable overlap of styles, and the spirit of the New Wave is more embracing than it is particular. For example, Robert Webber wrote of seven contemporary worship styles: liturgical, traditional Protestant, creative, charismatic, praise-and-worship, convergence, and seekers' service/believers' worship.[6]

C. Michael Hawn in 2010 identified seven different "streams" of hymnody[7] currently identifiable, although individual examples may show influences of more than one source. These streams are Roman Catholic Liturgical Renewal Hymnody; Protestant Contemporary Classical Hymnody; African American Spirituals and Gospel Songs; Revival/Gospel Songs; Folk Song Influences; Pentecostal Songs; and Global and Ecumenical Song Forms.

There is, to be sure, still a mainstream practice which owes its direction to Luther, Watts, and the Wesleys, often incorporating gospel songs by Sankey, Bliss, and their followers. In some conservative, and particularly

---

[5] Webber was the author of the influential *Worship Is a Verb* (Word Publishers, 1985)

[6] Robert Webber, "Seven Styles of Morning Worship," *The Complete Library of Christian Worship*, vol. 3 (Nashville: Star Song, 1994), pp. 111-27.

[7] Hawn, "Streams of Song," pp. 18-19.

Southern, churches convention songs which followed them are popular. The commercial Christian songs of Mosie Lister, Bill Gaither, Twila Paris, Dennis Jernigan, and others have a secure place, and the Christian music industry is an important source for new congregational song. The efficiency with which new songs can be disseminated through modern media is challenged by the magnitude of newly created repertoire.

There may be a new call for accountability in the Christian music community. Nathan Myrick, in "Double Authenticity: Celebrity, Consumption, and the Christian Worship Music Industry,"[8] writes that the "Celebrity Model" of worship performer, such as those just mentioned, is being replaced by an expectation for performer/composers to document their commitment by their affiliation with, participation in, and leadership among a particular congregational fellowship.

---

[8] *The Hymn*, Vol. 69, No. 2, Spring 2018, pp. 21-27.

CHAPTER 13

THE FUTURE OF CONGREGATIONAL SINGING

Will the next generation of congregational singers see changes as significant as those of recent history? Perhaps our music will continue to become less formal and more improvisational. Perhaps it will continue to track features of popular and commercial music. Will churches be singing Christian rap? Will they sing along with projected video performances? Will the pendulum swing back toward the traditional repertoire? In this section we will consider some of the factors that help to determine our preferences and practices.

Why do we sing?

James wrote (5:1) that singing psalms is an appropriate way to express one's joy. Paul (Colossians 3:16, Ephesians 5:19) said that we teach and admonish each other while singing psalms, hymns, and spiritual songs; but he also included an internal component, reminding us that we make melody in our hearts. The psalms, hymns, and spiritual songs of the early church were mostly about praise; but they were aimed laterally and inwardly as much as vertically, if we might use directional metaphors. In other words, songs of praise were directed to God — but not only to God. They were also sung with and to each other as well as being encouraging to the singer.

As Reformation leaders introduced songs that commented on struggles and encouraged perseverance, these vertical, horizontal, and inward directions still applied, as they do today. We sing to God, because our connection with him is our lifeline, at the core of our being. But we also sing to each other and to ourselves. As we sing, we establish our relationships and our intent — we are God's — we are each other's — we are committed.

Congregational singing has been assigned a primary role, perhaps **the** primary role, in many evangelical church meetings today. When inviting others to visit their church, members often brag on the quality of the music, reporting that it provides their favorite moments of the service. Darryl Tippens writes with missionary zeal in his booklet *That's Why We Sing: Reclaiming the Wonder of Congregational Singing*.[1] According to Tippens, singing is important for a number of reasons:
 •Singing Connects Us To God;
 •Singing Changes Us;
 •Singing Inspires Faith;
 •Singing Connects Head and Heart, Body and Soul;
 •Singing Connects Us To One Another;
 •Singing Proclaims the Good News.

If we were to expand the realm of examination beyond the spiritual area, we might add at least two additional observations:
 •Singing Is Fun;
 •Singing Is Artistically Rewarding.
Additionally, congregational singing is the only activity in some conservative congregations in which women are allowed to publicly participate.

Singing plays multiple roles in our lives. We sing our alma maters, our national anthems, our fight songs, our children's songs, our alphabet songs, our silly songs, our art songs, our youthful rebellion songs, our love songs, our inspirational songs, our fun songs, our dance songs, our nostalgic songs — and the list goes on and on. So if we were to ask the question "Why do we sing?" we would have to qualify it with the response "Why do we sing **what**?"

And the same is true with our church music. We sing different songs, at different times, in different places, and for different reasons. Some songs are extraordinarily beautiful. Some remind us of our home congregation, or of our parents or grandparents. Some are emotionally stirring. Some are motivational or inspirational. Some are comforting. Some are packed with praise. Some are fun. Some have thrilling music.

Singing has an uncommon richness because it speaks in two languages: the language of words and the language of music. It's that second language

---

[1] Abilene: Leafwood Press, 2007.

that uniquely opens the doors of the heart and enables us to express and receive seemingly transcendent ideas.

The role of music

This bilingual nature of song alarmed Augustine, who feared that he might be more attentive to the music than to the words. And it was the attractiveness of music that led John Wesley in 1768 to warn about Methodist songs that were more entertaining than devout. Others expressed similar concerns, including Athanasius, Luther, Zwingli, Calvin, John Knox, the Council of Trent, and Alexander Campbell. They might propose the "recitation test," which suggests that we determine the quality of a song by reciting the text without music.

Can music really become a hindrance rather than a support for our praise? There's an old song that says, "Falling in love with love is falling for make-believe," warning against confusing the object of our affections with the affections themselves. Is it also possible that one might fall in love with the forms of worship rather than with God? Might we think we have been drawn especially close to God when in reality we have simply really enjoyed the musical experience?

On the other hand, it can be asserted that music is — in and of itself, even without words — a way of communicating our praise to God and our encouragement to each other. This sentiment is expressed in the contemporary song "Listen to Our Hearts," which explains, "But words are not enough to tell you of our love, so listen to our hearts."[2] There may be an early reference to non-verbal praise and communion in Paul's account of praying and singing in the spirit.[3] The idea that music itself is an exalted form of expression is not unique to evangelicals. Arnold Schopenhauer, the nineteenth-century German philosopher, believed that music provided man's closest connection with the Universal Will. He held that since

---

[2] Steven Curtis Chapman and Geoff Moore. Copyright ©1994 Sparrow Song/Peach Hill Songs/Songs on the Forefront/Administered by EMI Christian Music Publishing

[3] I Corinthians 14:15. Note that Paul describes his tongue speaking as a private matter, not to be shared in an assembly without a spiritually gifted interpreter's participation. He asserts that in the assembly he would rather say five words with meaning than ten thousand words in a tongue.

wordless music was the most abstract and least earth-bound of the arts it was, consequently, the most transcendent and ennobling.[4]

Two ironies

This discussion of the place of music in congregational song introduces a great irony: congregational singing, which many cite as significant in producing a sense of community, is also a leading cause of dissonance among us. Music has become important in our churches, and people have different musical preferences. While music has brought joy and unity, it has also brought complaints, migration to other churches, and divided congregations..

We may note another irony involving the role of music. In the early church, music was added to a text in order to lend it dignity and attention. A text that was intoned gained more respectful attention than one simply spoken. That may not still be true.

Imagine, for example, a congregation at prayer, in which a leader is saying, "Lord, we praise you, we lift up your name, we love to praise you, because you came to show us how to live; you died for us and were buried; and you were raised in glory. We praise you!" What is the expected demeanor of those present? All would be respectful, perhaps with bowed heads, perhaps with raised heads and raised arms. There would be no conversations and no casual attitudes.

What if however, the same congregation were singing this song by Rick Founds?

Lord, I lift your name on high, Lord, I love to sing your praises;
I'm so glad you're in my life, I'm so glad you came to save us.
You came from heaven to earth to show the way,
from the earth to the cross, my debt to pay;
from the cross to the grave, from the grave to the sky.
Lord, I lift your name on high!"[5] (PftL 953)

While the general demeanor would be attentive, it is likely that people would feel free to slide into a pew as a latecomer, to greet others around

---

[4] *The World as Will and Representation*, pp. 448ff.

5 Copyright © 1984 by Maranatha! Music.

them, or to have a brief conversation with a friend. Is it possible that the addition of music might actually detract from our attention to the words?

Instrumental music and musical style

A number of instruments are mentioned in Old Testament in connection with Jewish worship. The trumpet was probably used, as was the *shofar*, as a means of signaling, of warning, or of calling to assembly. Trumpets were common in the ancient world; a golden trumpet was found in the tomb of King Tutankhanen (d.1323 B.C.). The instrument sometimes referred to as a "pipe" or "flute" was actually an expressive reed instrument similar to the aulos associated with the Grecian Dionysian cult. The lyre and the harp were for those with more refined tastes. In Greece they were associated with Apollo, the god of light and beauty. They were plucked rather than strummed and were probably used to provide pitches for singers or to play in alternation with vocal melody. Drums and cymbals accompanied processions and dances.

Though they were used in Jewish, Grecian, Roman, and Egyptian temples and cultic events, there is no indication that instruments were used in early Christian meetings. As we discussed in Chapter 1, this is not because they were proscribed. They were simply irrelevant; there was no purpose for them. There was no ceremonial role for an instrument, and the singers were not professional bards who would require lyres for their performances.

In the third and fourth centuries objections to the use of instruments begin to appear in Christian writings, indicating that some were introducing instruments into public or private worship. But unaccompanied singing remained the standard practice in churches until the seventeenth century; it was validated during the Catholic Council of Trent (1545-63) and was the mode preferred by most church reformers.[6]

When one considers all church practices, in all times, in all Christian fellowships, in all parts of the world, those who use instruments in church have been in the minority. A cappella singing is still the predominant mode in Orthodox churches and in a handful of other groups. However, in most

---

[6] For a lengthy roster of those who have argued against the use of instrumental music in church, see Price's *Old Light on New Worship*, pp. 67-140.

denominations today a cappella singing has become an uncommon practice, and many people are surprised to hear that there are those who have
objections to instrumental music in church.

How did this happen? How can it be that the early church never considered using instruments while most contemporary groups rarely consider
doing without them?

The answers are found in the enhanced role that music has claimed in the
Christian church. Whereas in the ancient church music was merely the
servant of the text, a vehicle, it has continued to receive increased attention as the years passed. To advance the metaphor, the vehicle that once
was a cart is now a Ferrari, once just a mode of conveyance, now a main
attraction of the journey.

In the centuries following the establishment of Christianity as the state
religion, magnificence of architecture, art, and music came to be seen as
validation of the church's authority; and of the power and prestige of the
local bishop and ruler. Churches vied to build the largest cathedral, to hire
the most talented musicians, and to develop the most impressive musical sonorities. The first church to attract international attention because
of its music was Notre Dame in Paris, under the leadership of the choir-
masters Leonin and Perotin (late twelfth and early thirteenth centuries).
As medieval church musicians explored more elaborate musical styles, it
was natural to use an organ to support one or more voices, and the organ
and other instruments gradually came to speak independently. Giovanni
Gabrieli's vocal and instrumental church music brought admiration to the
city of Venice and to its rulers around 1600, and musicians traveled great
distances to hear and imitate it.

As Renaissance reformers re-introduced congregational singing, they
generally sought to lessen the significance of music in relation to text.
They were united in their preference for a cappella performance, and for a
time Protestant psalmody and hymnody was sung to fairly simple music.
This began to change around the turn of the eighteenth century as tunes
became more complex and artistic, often implying a requirement of basic
instrumental accompaniment. By the end of that century, Methodist congregations were requiring tunes that were robust and entertaining.

A different sort of musical statement came with the repetition, rhythmic emphasis, and clever musical devices continued with the camp-meeting tunes, often based on folk and dance music, and quite amenable to accompaniment by fiddle or banjo.

Along with the changes in vocal style, organs came to be considered as necessary in the more affluent nineteenth-century Protestant churches; pianos were adopted in the early twentieth century; and other instruments followed. It was a natural and pervasive development.

The expectation of instruments in Christian music has led some non-instrumental performance groups to create virtual vocal bands, complete with the sounds of electric bass, percussion, strings, and brass — but still "legal" because the sounds are produced non-instrumentally. And in a similar, though not identical, development, convention songs resulted in works like the Stamps/Baxter "He Bore It All" (PftL 820), which features melody accompanied by vocal syncopation in the style of the period's instrumental marches. The singers do not imitate instrumental sounds, but the music of the songs imitates instrumental rhythmic effects.

Reconsidering the texts

When Paul writes of "psalms, hymns, and spiritual songs," he is referring to texts and not to musical genres or tunes. We organize by different categories today, and when we speak of spirituals, gospel songs, convention songs, hymns, youth songs, or praise and worship songs, we generally refer to musical styles.

Marshall McLuhan wrote in 1964, "The medium is the message."[7] His observation might be applied to congregational singing, in that our mere participation in it can be more important than the actual words or notes we sing. It is as though we put our songs into a common sacramental container and pull from that container without discrimination. In other words: a minister may ask a worship leader at some point during a service to "lead us in a song" or to "give us some music" without specifying whether the intent is praise, prayer, encouragement, or celebration,. The implication is that all songs are essentially alike. Or a leader may announce, "Now let us

---

[7] *Understanding Media: The Extensions of Man*. New York: McGraw-Hill, 1964.

praise God in song," when the congregation is actually preparing to sing a song of encouragement or prayer.

In fact, the texts of our songs are different in content, intent, and address. Sometimes we sing praise, sometimes prayer, sometimes celebration, sometimes encouragement, sometimes meditation. Sometimes we sing of our current state, sometimes of our longings and intent. Sometimes we sing to God; sometimes we sing to those around us; sometimes we primarily sing to ourselves.

Communication styles change with time. While Luther, Watts, the Wesleys, Newton, and Keble were accustomed to lengthy explications and elaborations, we live today in an era of succinct prose, 280-character communication, and short attention spans; and our contemporary Christian music reflects those characteristics. Many reject older hymns because they have "too many words" and require too much processing, preferring gospel and convention songs with refrains or contemporary songs with short repeated texts.

The story continues

The story of congregational singing is a rich and diverse one, beginning with the songs of praise that are left to us from the early church. As heresies threatened, texts were set to music to teach and promote orthodox doctrine.

Reformation leaders used songs to buttress faith and to inspire perseverance in the face of persecution. These were commonly sung to simple melodies until music began to be introduced that was more complex, entertaining, sentimental, and rhythmic, and the focus of congregational singing gradually shifted from texts to tunes.

This story does not follow a simple track. Filled with evolution, revolution, and innovation, it tells of those who have tried desperately to preserve tradition and old forms, and of those who have turned away from the old in favor of new modes of expression.

As we write our own chapters in this history, we share in the diversity that we have observed in the past. Many of us are uncritically content to do whatever is prescribed by church and worship leaders, holding to Pope's assumption that "whatever is, is right."[8] Some are determined to adhere to that which is comfortable and familiar, and some encourage change for the sake of change. Others, convinced that an encounter with the transcendent God must itself be transcendent, explore new modes and styles in search of a "meaningful worship experience." This search permeates religious history and is the subject of John Greenleaf Whittier's poem in the second appendix.

The story of congregational song is our ancestors', and it is ours. As to what will happen in the future — those chapters are still being written and sung, and the reverberations are heard in the voices and hearts of God's servants everywhere, as we teach, admonish and encourage each other and give praise to our God and Savior.

---

[8] Alexander Pope, "An Essay on Man: Epistle 1"

WHAT HAPPENS IN THE CONGREGATION

A s its title implies, this book has taken us on a limited journey
through part of the history of congregational singing. If we were
to investigate the whole of Christendom we would encounter an
incredible diversity of practices, given the differences between denominations, countries, ethnicities, languages, political environments, traditions,
and cultures. And yet all of these ultimately emanate from a common
source — the followers of Christ who first began regularly gathering
nearly two thousand years ago.

It seems appropriate as we conclude this study to briefly look at the nature
of those early assemblies, to see if they offer any helpful models or suggestions for us today. Change is inevitable, but it is not always beneficial
unless properly directed. Discovering and developing more effective types
of interactions in our meetings can help us to set our course toward greater
spiritual growth, and the practices of the early church are valuable in that
investigation.

Meetings in the early church and today

In the New Testament there are only three passages that describe Christian
meetings. The earliest tells of the young church in Jerusalem (Acts 2:42-
47, 4:23-31, 5:11-13, 42). The new Christians, understandably, attended to
the teachings of the apostles, who frequented Solomon's Colonnade in the
Temple Court. But they also met daily in small groups in private homes,
they prayed, they broke bread and ate together. Because there were so
many visitors in the city, locals provided food and necessities, even to the
point of selling their own properties and possessions (Acts 4:32-35).

The next reference to an early assembly is in Acts 20:7-12, where we read
of Paul's meeting with the church in Troas. He arrived on a Monday and

stayed for an entire week, presumably because the church gathered only on Sunday nights. They arranged to meet in a well-lit third story room, where Paul talked with them until midnight, after which they broke bread.

The most complete, and intriguing, early account of a Christian assembly comes from Paul's first letter (ca. A.D. 55) to the church in Corinth that he had established about three years earlier and that he had nurtured in person for at least eighteen months. This group suffered from divisiveness, competition, doctrinal misunderstandings, and blatant immorality.

From this letter (I Corinthians 11-14) we deduce that they met around suppertime and that each member or family brought food and drink which they were expected to share as they "broke bread" in a combination Lord's Supper and fellowship meal.[1] Some of the poorer members, perhaps arriving late because of their work, were dependent on the wealthier to provide for them, and some of the early arrivals had already drunk and eaten their fill, leaving nothing to be shared. Paul indignantly observed that this meal was intended to remind participants of the Lord's body, which was sacrificed for his followers, and that those who failed to attend to the unity and the needs of this body of believers were obviously inattentive to the meaning of the sacrifice. The Corinthians' communal meal had taken on characteristics of a common Greek *symposium*, or drinking party!

The meeting deteriorated in other ways after the meal. Through the laying on of Paul's hands, God had given a number of them spiritual gifts that were remarkable; in some cases, spectacular. One of these was the ability to speak in spiritual languages, uttering messages that could not be understood without the intervention of a similarly gifted interpreter, and some were abusing that gift by employing it improperly. Some who did not actually have the gift may have claimed it in order to assert their own spiritual superiority. Some women were playing an improper role. The results, as seen in I Corinthians 14:27-40, could be disorderly, competitive, and divisive.

Paul reminded them that the highest quality of the church is love (in chapter 13, the famous "love chapter"), which required honoring and attending to the needs of each other, and that the purpose of their gathering was

---

[1] The model supper which Jesus celebrated with his disciples was a combination of dinner and commemoration — Matthew 26, Mark 14, Luke 22, John 14.

edification (14:12, 26). He deemphasized the role of spiritual languages, because they were edifying only under certain circumstances.

That concludes the descriptions in the New Testament of early meetings, and although we do not find a common formal pattern we do find consistent content, which included edification, encouragement, instruction, a shared commemorative meal, and praise. Second-century accounts from Pliny and Justin Martyr (see Chapter 1, "Early Christian Singing") confirm this observation. As the church spread throughout the world, this content remained constant, although it might take different forms.

Mutual interaction and individual participation were vital to the development of the church. We saw that in Paul's letter (I Corinthians 14:26): "What then shall we say, brothers and sisters? When you come together, each of you has a hymn, or a word of instruction, a revelation, a tongue or an interpretation. Everything must be done so that the church may be built up." He gave special emphasis to this individual responsibility in his letter to the Ephesians (4:7-16), saying, "**to each one of us** grace has been given as Christ apportioned it…so that the body of Christ may be built up. …we will in all things grow up into him who is the Head, that is, Christ. From him the whole body, joined and held together by every supporting ligament, grows and **builds itself up** in love, as **each part does its work**." And the writer of Hebrews (10:24-25) instructed readers to, "consider how we may spur one another on toward love and good deeds, not giving up meeting together, as some are in the habit of doing, but encouraging one another." The weekly assembly provided the opportunity for mutual strengthening, encouragement, and admonition. It was crucial to the growth of the body and of its members.

Smaller congregations encourage individual responsibility, and during the first three centuries of the church's history its gatherings were limited by the size of the meeting place and the nature of the fellowship meal. Many groups met in homes or in halls which could not accommodate large numbers. The changes were dramatic when the meal was later reduced to small portions of bread and wine and the Roman church began to meet in large basilicas.

We live in a different world than that of the early Christians, with different expectations of what a church meeting should look like. Depending on our background and preferences, we may anticipate fine music and singing, whether congregational or provided by designated musical groups; re-spectable church buildings, with classrooms, recreational areas, food preparation facilities, good sound systems, and wi-fi; a regular schedule of church meetings, with predictable content and structure; hired support and ministerial staff to oversee, instruct, counsel, and serve; an engaging preacher; adequate parking; and procedures to assure communication and planning.

Our congregations tend to be relatively large, and many attendees are accustomed to sitting in a pew, participating in (or listening to) group singing, hearing a sermon and prayers, and departing without having any significant interaction with another person. The mutual engagement modeled in early church meetings does not happen in these circumstances. Without personal relationships and engagement, congregational singing and pew sitting are essentially anonymous activities, and the body doesn't function well when its members are not identified and tasked.

Given our current circumstances, how do we design meetings that retain the central content that was vital to the early church and is still required for our growth as Christians? How do we encourage individual members to be personally involved in edification and encouragement, to play their parts in giving and receiving instruction, to fully participate in a shared commemorative meal, and to praise? How do the challenges facing us today compare with those faced by the early church, and how do we deal with those challenges as a body? And what role does singing play in help-ing us to grow individually and collectively? These are some of the ques-tions we cannot ignore.

The Christian's audience

Søren Kierkegaard's allegory of the theater[2] offers an interesting insight into the intended reason for our meetings. Most of us, asked to compare a worship service to the theater, would say that we are the performers and that our singing and praying is directed toward God.

Kierkegaard agrees that we are the performers and that God is the au-dience. But in his allegory, the weekly meeting is a time for leaders

---

[2] Søren Kierkegaard, *Purity of Heart Is to Will One Thing*, trans. Douglas V. Steere, New York: Harper & Brothers Publishers, 1948, pp. 180-82.

("prompters") to remind us of our lines. The performance takes place **after** we leave the meeting, as God observes us play the role of his followers ministering to the world. The assembly is the rehearsal; life is the performance.

Kierkegaard's perspective is important. We do not go to church to perform for God. Instead we go to be reminded of our lines and actions during the time of the real performance, which takes place during the rest of the week. We gather to support each other in our roles, offering encouragement and assistance as needed.

Nor do we go to church so that we can leave the cares and struggles of the world outside. It is in our meetings that we share those cares and struggles and equip ourselves — and each other — to successfully meet our challenges when we leave.

If the purpose of our assemblies echoes that of the meetings of the early church, they will be designed to prepare us to live in a way that delights the Audience of One.

CEREMONY AND SERVICE

John Greenleaf Whittier's (1807-92) "The Brewing of Soma" (1872) provides an interesting reflection on mankind's search for experiential worship. Whittier, a Quaker, cites examples of man's historic inclination to approach deity through extravagant ceremonies and rituals, after which he proposes an alternative type of engagement.

This issue is not incidental or irrelevant. How do we worship? In the absence of immediate feedback from our God, how do we know that we have satisfied our need and his request to praise him? How do mortal humans interact with the incomprehensible transcendent?

We all answer these questions in different ways. For some the encounter requires ceremony, heightened emotions, and dramatic experiences.. For Whittier it demands a life of contemplation and service. His poem offers an artful survey of humanity's attempts to encounter deity.

The fagots[1] blazed, the caldron's smoke
Up through the green wood curled;
"Bring honey from the hollow oak,
Bring milky sap," the brewers spoke,
In the childhood of the world.

And brewed they well or brewed they ill,
The priests thrust in their rods,
First tasted, and then drank their fill,
And shouted, with one voice and will,
"Behold the drink of gods!"

---

[1] A bundle of sticks or twigs tied together for firewood

They drank, and lo! in heart and brain
A new, glad life began;
The gray of hair grew young again,
The sick man laughed away his pain,
The cripple leaped and ran.

"Drink, mortals, what the gods have sent,
Forget your long annoy."
So sang the priests. From tent to tent
The Soma's sacred madness went,
A storm of drunken joy.

Then knew each rapt inebriate
A winged and glorious birth,
Soared upward, with strange joy elate,
Beat, with dazed head, Varuna's gate,
And, sobered, sank to earth.

The land with Soma's praises rang;
On Gihon's banks of shade
Its hymns the dusky maidens sang;
In joy of life or mortal pang
All men to Soma prayed.

The morning twilight of the race
Sends down these matin psalms;
And still with wondering eyes we trace
The simple prayers to Soma's grace,
That Vedic verse embalms.

As in that child-world's early year,
Each after age has striven
By music, incense, vigils drear,
And trance, to bring the skies more near,
Or lift men up to heaven!

Some fever of the blood and brain,
Some self-exalting spell,
The scourger's keen delight of pain,
The Dervish dance, the Orphic strain,
The wild-haired Bacchant's yell,

The desert's hair-grown hermit sunk
The saner brute below;
The naked Santon, hashish-drunk,
The cloister madness of the monk,
The fakir's torture-show!

And yet the past comes round again,
And new doth old fulfil;
In sensual transports wild as vain
We brew in many a Christian fane
The heathen Soma still!

Dear Lord and Father of mankind,
Forgive our foolish ways!
Reclothe us in our rightful mind,
In purer lives Thy service find,
In deeper reverence, praise.

In simple trust like theirs who heard
Beside the Syrian sea
The gracious calling of the Lord,
Let us, like them, without a word,
Rise up and follow Thee.

O Sabbath rest by Galilee!
O calm of hills above,
Where Jesus knelt to share with Thee
The silence of eternity
Interpreted by love!

With that deep hush subduing all
Our words and works that drown
The tender whisper of Thy call,
As noiseless let Thy blessing fall
As fell Thy manna down.

Drop Thy still dews of quietness,
Till all our strivings cease;
Take from our souls the strain and stress,
And let our ordered lives confess
The beauty of Thy peace.

Breathe through the heats of our desire
Thy coolness and Thy balm;
Let sense be dumb, let flesh retire;
Speak through the earthquake, wind, and fire,
O still, small voice of calm!

Selective Bibliography

Bailey, Albert Edward. *The Gospel in Hymns*. New York: Charles Scribner's Sons, 1950.

Blume, Friedrich. *Protestant Church Music: A History*. New York: W. W. Norton & Company, Inc., 1974.

Christ-Janer, Albert; Charles W. Hughes; and Carleton Sprague Smith. *American Hymns Old and New*. New York: Columbia University Press, 1980.

Davison, Archibald T. and Willi Apel. *Historical Anthology of Music*. Cambridge: Harvard University Press, 1949.

Douglas, Winfred. *Church Music in History & Practice*. Revised with additional material by Leonard Ellinwood. New York: Charles Scribner's Sons, 1962.

Epp, Maureen and Carol Ann Weaver. *Sound in the Land: Essays on Monnonites and Music*. Kitchener, Ontario: Pandora Press, 2005.

Eskew, Harry and Hugh T. McElrath. *Sing with Understanding: An Introduction to Christian Hymnology*. Second Edition, Revised and Expanded. Nashville, Tenn.: Church Street Press, 1995.

Ferguson, Everett. *Early Christians Speak*. Austin, Tex.: Sweet Publishing, 1971.

Griggs, John Cornelius. "The Church Music of Two Centuries." Programme and Addresses Delivered at the One Hundred and Fiftieth Anniversary of the First Congregational Church, Bristol, Conn., October 12th, 1897.

Hamilton, Michael S. "A Generation Changes North American Hymnody." *The Hymn*, Vol. 52, No. 3, July 2001, pp. 11-21.

Hawn, C. Michael. "Streams of Song: An overview of congregational song in the twenty-first century." *The Hymn*, Vol. 61, No. 1, Winter 2010, pp. 16-26.

Hehn, Jonathan. "Congregational Song as Theological Debate in Late Antiquity: A Case Study of Arius's Thalia and the Development of Trinitarian Orthodoxy." *The Hymn*, Vol. 65, No. 1, Winter 2014, pp. 13-20.

Hustad, Donald P. *Jubilate II: Church Music in Worship and Renewal*. Carol Stream, Ill.: Hope Publishing Company, 1993.

Hustad, Donald P. *True Worship: Recovering the Wonder and Majesty*. Shaw Books, 2000.

Idelsohn, A. Z. *Jewish Music in its Historical Development*. New York: Tudor Publishing Company, 1948.

Josselyn-Cranson, Heather. "Gaining a New Appreciation for Calvin and Music: The Past, Present, and Future of the Genevan Psalm Tune." *The Hymn*, Vol. 63, No. 3, Summer 2012, pp. 22-28.

Leaver, Robin A. "The Failure that Succeeded: The *New Version* of Tate and Brady." *The Hymn*, Vol. 48, No. 4, October 1997, pp. 22-31.

Lorenz, Ellen Jane. *Glory, Hallelujah! The Story of the Campmeeting Spiritual*. Nashville, Tenn.: Abington, 1980.

Mankin, Jim. "Alexander Campbell's Contributions to Hymnody." *The Hymn*, Vol. 49, No. 1, January 1998, pp. 10-14.

Mankin, Jim. "L. O. Sanderson, Church of Christ Hymn Writer." *The Hymn*, Vol. 42, No. 1, January 1995, pp. 27-31.

Martin, Ralph P. *Worship in the Early Church*. Grand Rapids: William B. Eerdmans Publishing Company, 1964.

McKinnon, James. *Music in Early Christian Literature*. New York: Cambridge University Press, 1987.

Music, David W. *Hymnology: A Collection of Source Readings*. Lanham, Md.: The Scarecrow Press, Inc., 1996.

Myrick, Nathan. "Double Authenticity: Celebrity, Consumption, and the Christian Worship Music Industry." *The Hymn*, Vol. 69, No. 2, Spring 2018, pp. 21-27.

Parks, Edna. *The Hymns and Hymn Tunes Found in the English Metrical Psalters*. New York: Charles Scribner's Sons, 1966.

Price, John. *Old Light on New Worship: Musical Instruments and the Worship of God, a Theological, Historical, and Psychological Study*. Avinger, Tex.: Simpson Publishing Company, 2007.

Polachic, Raymond W. "Hymnic Illiteracy in the Pew." *The Hymn*, Vol. 42, No. 3, July 1991, pp. 37-38.

Quasten, Johannes. *Music & Worship in Pagan & Christian Antiquity*. Translated by Boniface Ramsey. Washington: National Association of Pastoral Musicians, 1983.

Reynolds, William J. and Milburn Price. *A Survey of Christian Hymnody*. Fourth Edition Revised and Enlarged By David W. Music and Milburn Price. Carol Stream, Ill.: Hope Publishing Company, 1999.

Routley, Erik. *An English-Speaking Hymnal Guide*. Collegeville, Minn.: The Liturgical Press, 1979.

Routley, Erik. *The Music of Christian Hymns*. Chicago: G.I.A. Publications, Inc., 1981.

Routley, Erik. *A Panorama of Christian Hymnody*. Chicago: G.I.A. Publications, Inc., 1979.

Sendrey, Alfred and Mildred Norton. David's Harp: *The Story of Music in Biblical Times*. New York: New American Library, 1964.

Stapert, Calvin R. *A New Song for an Old World: Musical Thought in the Early Church*. Grand Rapids, Michigan: William B Eerdmans Publishing Company, 2007.

Temperley, Nicholas and Stephen Banfield, editors. *Music and the Wesleys*. Urbana, Illinois: University of Illinois Press, 2010.

Tippens, Darryl. *That's Why We Sing: Reclaiming the Wonder of Congregational Singing*. Abilene, Texas: Leafwood Publishers, 2007.

Tripp, David H. and Peter Wheeler, "The Oldest Christian Hymn with Music: Its Use as a Seminary Project in Liturgical Studies." *The Hymn*, Vol. 48, No. 2, April 1997, pp. 20-24.

Tucker, Karen B. Westerfield. "Liturgical Perspectives on Changes in North American Hymnody in the Past Twenty-Five Years." *The Hymn*, Vol. 52, No. 3, July 2001, pp. 22-27.

Wainwright, Geoffrey and Karen B. Westerfield Tucker, editors. *The Oxford History of Christian Worship*. New York: Oxford University Press, 2006.

Westermayer, Paul. "The Future of Congregational Song." *The Hymn*, Vol. 46, No. 1, January 1995, pp. 4-9.

Wilson-Dickson, Andrew. *The Story of Christian Music*. Batavia, Ill.: Lion Publishing, 1991.

Young, Carlton R. *Companion to the United Methodist Hymnal*. Nashville: Abingdon Press, 1993.

INDEX

A

ABBEY 85
Achtliederbuch 34
Act of Uniformity 53
Agnus Dei 28
Ainsworth's Psalter 70
Akers, Doris 138
Alas! and Did My Savior Bleed 81
Alexander, Charles "Charlie" 129, 130
All Hail the Pow'r of Jesus' Name 99
All the Way My Savior Leads Me 131
Almost Persuaded 128
Amazing Grace 103
Ambrose 25
Am I a Soldier of the Cross? 85
Amish 44
AMSTERDAM 95
Anabaptists 32, 43, 44, 45, 47
And Can It Be That I Should Gain 95
And Did Those Feet in Ancient Time 121
Angels from the Realms of Glory 118
Anglo-Genevan Psalter 54, 58
Arianism 20, 23, 25
ARNSBERG 41
As the Deer 139
Athanasius 23, 26, 145
Augustine 25, 26, 145
Ausbund 44
Aus tiefer Not 34, 35

B

Bach, Johann Sebastian 37, 39, 42
Ballade meter 53
BALLERMA 112

baptismal hymn 12
Baptists 56
Basil 14
Baxter, J.R. 132
Bay Psalm Book 70
BEACH SPRING 112
Because He Lives 137
Beecher, Henry Ward 114, 137
Behold the Glories of the Lamb 79
Bernard of Clairvaux 29
Bernard of Cluny 29
Be With Me, Lord 136
Beza, Theodore 48, 49
Billings, William 107, 108
Bishop Lucas's Hymnal 31
Blake, William 121
Blessed Assurance 131
Blest Be the Tie That Binds 100
Bliss, Philip P. 128, 129, 131, 140
Bohemian Brethren 31, 44
Book of Common Prayer 52, 79, 98, 118, 120
Bourgeois, Louis 48, 49, 50, 57
Bradbury, William 127, 128, 131
Brady, Nicholas 66
Brethren (Anabaptist) 44, 45
Brewing of Soma, The 159–162
Bridges, Robert 121
Brighten the Corner Where You Are 130
Buried With Christ 136

C

Calvary Chapel 138
Calvin, Jean 47, 49, 50, 51, 52, 53, 57, 76, 145
Campbell, Alexander 110, 115, 145
Cane Ridge Revival 109
canticle 11
Cennick, John 99
Charge to Keep I Have, A 113
CHARITY 109, 112
Charlemagne 28
Children of the Heavenly King 99
Chisholm, Thomas 136
Christ Hymn 5
Christian Harmony 108
Christian Lyre 110
Christ Is Alive! 124
Christ the Lord Is Risen Today 95

CLEANSING FOUNTAIN 112
CLEARFIELD 128
Clement of Alexandria 14
Clement VII 52
Collection of Hymns for the Use of the People called Methodists, A 95
Collection of Psalms and Hymns, A 90
Come, Come, Ye Saints 115
Come, Let Us Join Our Cheerful Songs 85
Come, Thou Almighty King 99
Come, Thou Fount of Every Blessing 99
Come, Ye That Love the Lord 85
Common Meter 53, 65, 71
Common Tune 65
Constantine 20, 22, 28
contrafactum 38
Corde natus ex parentis 26
CORONATION 109
Council of Laodicea 23
Coverdale, Miles 52, 75
Cowper, William 100, 101, 103
Cranmer, Thomas 47, 52
Credo 28
Croft, William 68
Crosby, Fanny 130, 131
Crüger, Johann 40
CWM RHONDDA 121

D

Daman's Psalter 61
Day's Psalter 54
Dearmer, Percy 124
Deutscher Messe 37
Dicus, A.W. 133
Diocletian 19
Doane, William H. 131
Doddridge, Phillip 99
Domitian 19
Dorsey, Thomas A. 136
DUNDEE 64, 85
Dwight, Timothy 109
Dykes, John Bacchus 119, 120

E

EBENEZER 121
Edwards, Jonathan 98, 109
Edward VI 52, 53
Ein feste Burg 36

Elizabeth I 49, 54, 55, 70
English Hymnal, The 124
Este's Psalter 61, 70
Eternal Father, Strong to Save 120
Evangelical harp, The 110

F

Faith Is the Victory 129
Father, Hear the Prayer We Offer 120
Fawcett, John 100
For the Anniversary Day of One's Conversion 91
For the Fruit of All Creation 124
For You I Am Praying 129
Fosdick, Harry Emerson 136
FOUNDATION 112
Foundery Collection 95
Francis of Assisi 29
Franklin, Benjamin 98
Frederick the Wise 33

G

Gabriel, Charles 130, 136
Gabrieli, Giovanni 148
Gaither, Bill 137, 138, 141
Gardiner, William 118
Genevan Psalter 48, 51, 57
Giardini, Felice de 99
Gloria 15, 28
Glorious Things of Thee Are Spoken 103
Glory Song 130
Glory to God, and praise and love 91
God Himself is With Us 41
God Is the Fountain Whence 113
God moves in a mysterious way 103
God of Grace and God of Glory 136
Go, Labor On 113
Goostly Psalms and Spirituall Songes 52
Gospel Hymns and Sacred Songs 128, 129
Goudimel, Claude 49, 50, 51
Great Awakening 98, 107, 109
Great Awakening of 1857 127
Great Is Thy Faithfulness 136
Great Persecution 19
Great Revival 109, 110
Green, Fred Pratt 124
Gregorian chant 29, 113

H

Hallelujah! What a Savior! 128
Handel, George Frideric 99
HANOVER 68
Hark how all the Welkin rings 93
Harkness, Robert 129
Head That Once Was Crowned with Thorns, The 119
Heber, Reginald 119
He Bore It All 132, 149
HE HIDETH MY SOUL 131
He Leadeth Me 128
Henry VIII 51, 53, 75
Herrnhut 87, 91
Holden, Oliver 109
Holy, Holy, Holy 119
HOLY MANNA 112
Homer 4
Hopkins, John 54
Horae Lyricae 79
How Can I Keep from Singing 131
How Glorious Are the Morning Stars 77
How Shall the Young Secure Their Hearts? 85
How Sweet the Name of Jesus Sounds 103
Huguenots 48
Hullah, John 118
Hus, Jan 31, 33, 46, 47
Hymns Ancient and Modern 120, 121
Hymns and Sacred Poems 93, 95
Hymns and Spiritual Songs 79

I

I Am Thine, O Lord 131
I Bring My Sins to Thee 129
I Come with Joy 124
I Gave My Life for Thee 129
I Love My Savior, Too 132
I Love Thy Kingdom, Lord 109, 113
I'm Not Ashamed to Own My Lord 85
In Christ Alone 139
Ingalls, Jeremiah 108, 109
Innsbruck, I Now Must Leave You 38
ITALIAN HYMN 99
It Is Well with My Soul 129

J

James I 65

Jernigan, Dennis 138, 141
Jerusalem 121
Jesu meine Freude 40
Jesus Christ Is Risen Today 69
Jesus Is Tenderly Calling Thee Home 131
Jesus, Lover of My Soul 95
Jesus Loves Me 128
Jesus, My All, to Heaven Is Gone 99
Jesus nimmt die Sünder an 42
Jesus, On the Mountain Peak 124
Jesus Shall Reign Where'er the Sun 82
Jesus, the Very Thought of Thee 29, 120
Joy to the World 82, 113
Just As I Am 128
Justin Martyr 8

K

Kaan, Fred 124
Keach, Benjamin 76, 77, 78
Keble, John 120, 150
Kelly, Thomas 119
KENOSIS 129
KINGSFOLD 125
Kirkpatrick, William 131, 136
Knox, John 58, 145
Kyrie 28

L

Lafferty, Karen 138
Lamb of God 138
Lasst uns erfreuen 40
Last Trumpet, The 111
Lead, Kindly Light 120
LEAD ME TO CALVARY 131
Leo III 28
Leo X 32, 52
Let the Lower Lights Be Burning 128
lining out 66, 114
Lister, Mosie 138, 141
Loblied 44
Lo! He Comes with Clouds Descending 99
London Songbook 87
Lord, Dismiss Us with Thy Blessing 100
LORD I'M COMING HOME 131
Lord my shepherd is, The 84
Lord to me a shepherd is, The 72
Love Divine, All Loves Excelling 95

Lowry, Robert 131
Luther, Martin 32–39, 41, 43, 46, 47, 51, 52
LUX BENIGNA 120
Lyon, James 106

M

Magnificat 11
Mainzer, Joseph 118
Marot, Clement 47, 48, 53
Mary I 53, 54
Mason, Lowell 113
Massachusetts Bay Colony 70
Mather, Cotton 73, 105
McGranahan, James 129
MELITA 120
Mennonites 44, 45
Methodist Hymnal 136
Methodists 89, 96, 99, 110, 118, 120, 127, 145, 148
MILES LANE 100
Moody, Dwight L. 128–130
Moravians 87, 89, 90, 91, 99
More Holiness Give Me 128
My Faith Looks Up to Thee 113
My Hope Is Built on Nothing Less 128
My Shepherd will supply my need 83

N

Neale, John Mason 120
Neander, Joachim 41
Nearer, My God, to Thee 113
Nearer the Cross 131
Nero 19
Neumeister, Erdmann 42
NEW BRITAIN 104, 111
New England Psalm Book 72
New England Psalm Singer 107
Newman, John Henry 120
New Song, The 132
Newton, John 100, 103
NICAEA 119, 120
Nicene Council and Creed 20, 28, 119
Niceta of Remesiana 97
Ninety and Nine, The 129
NORTHFIELD 108
Nunc dimittis 48
Nun danket alle Gott 40
Nystrom, Martin 139

O

O brother man 135
O Christ, the Healer 124
O! for a closer walk with God 102
O for a Thousand Tongues to Sing 95
Of the Father's Love Begotten 26
O get your hearts in order 111
Oglethorpe, James 89
O God, Thou bottomless abyss 90
OLD HUNDRED 57, 106
Old Version 54, 63, 70
Olney Hymns 100, 119
Only in Thee 136
O Sacred Head, Now Wounded 29, 38
O TO BE LIKE THEE 131
Our God, He Is Alive 133
Our God, Our Help in Ages Past 82
Oxford Book of Carols 124
Oxford Movement 114, 121
Oxyrhynchus hymn 15, 16

P

Paris, Twila 138, 141
Parker, Archbishop Matthew 59, 60
Parker's Psalter 59
Pass Me Not, O Gentle Savior 131
pentatonic hymn tunes 111, 112
Perronet, Edward 99, 100
Pietism 41, 87, 139
Playford, Henry 66
Playford, John 66, 72
Pliny 7
Plymouth Collection of Hymns and Tunes 114
Plymouth Colony 56, 70
Praise Him, Praise Him 131
Praise the Lord 113
Praise to the Lord, the Almighty 41
Precious Lord, Take My Hand 136
Proper tunes 64, 65
Prudentius 26
Psalms, Hymns, and Spiritual Songs 115
Psalms of David imitated 82
Psalterium Americanum 73
Purcell, Henry 67
Puritans 55, 56, 71

R

Ravenscroft's Psalter 63, 64, 71
Ravenscroft, Thomas 63, 64, 66
REDEEMED 131
Rescue the Perishing 131
Robinson, Robert 99
Rodeheaver, Homer 129, 130

S

Sacred Harp 113, 115
Sacred Melody 97
Safe in the Arms of Jesus 131
Salvation Has Been Brought Down 132
Sanctus 28
Sanderson, Lloyd O. 136
Sankey, Ira D. 128, 129, 130, 131, 140
Sappho 4
Scottish Psalter 58, 59
Second Great Awakening 110
Seek Ye First 138
Select Hymns with Tunes Annext 95
Selection of Hymns from the best authors, A 100
Selection of Psalms and Hymns for Public and Private Use, A 118
Selina, Countess of Huntingdon 99
Shakers 114, 115
Shall We Gather at the River 131
Shelter in the Time of Storm 129
Shepherd of Tender Youth 14
Shrubsole, William 100
Simple Gifts 115
Simply Trusting 129
SINE NOMINE 124
Sing and Be Happy 132
Sing Me a Song About Jesus 132
Sing to the Lord with joyful voice 82
Sinners Jesus Will Receive 129
Soldiers of Christ, Arise! 95
Something Beautiful 137
Songs of Praise 124
Southern Harmony 111, 112
SOUTHWELL 85
Spafford, Horatio 129
Spener, Philip Jakob 41, 87
Splendor paternae gloriae 25
ST. AGNES 120
Stamps, Virgil O. 132, 137
ST. ANNE 67, 81, 85

Sternhold and Hopkins 53, 54, 56, 58, 61, 70
Sternhold, Thomas 53, 54
Still, Still with Thee 129
ST. JAMES 75
ST. MAGNUS 85
Stone, Barton W. 109, 115
ST. SYLVESTER 120
Sunday School songs 128
Sun of My Soul, Thou Savior Dear 120
Sweet Hour of Prayer 128
Sweet, Sweet Spirit 138
syllabic style 18

T

TALLIS' CANON 60, 85, 95
Tallis, Thomas 60
Tate and Brady Psalter 68, 75
Tate, Nahum 66, 67, 75
Te Deum 24
Tersteegen, Gerhard 41
Thank You 138
Theodosius 22
There's Something About That Name 137
Thirty Years' War 40
Thou Hidden Love of God 41
'TIS SO SWEET TO TRUST IN JESUS 131
To God Be the Glory 131
Toplady, Augustus 99
To Us a Child of Hope Is Born 113
Tractarian Movement 120
Trajan 7
Tufts, John 105
Tyndale, William 52

U

Under His Wings 129
Unitas Fratrum 31
Upon the Banks of Jordan Stood 115
Urania 106

V

Vaughan, James D. 132, 137
Vaughan Williams, Ralph 40, 60, 124
VILLE DU HAVRE 129
VOLLER WUNDER 42

W

Walter, Johann 37
WAREHAM 85
Watts, Isaac 34, 78–85, 90, 91, 98, 99, 109, 111, 131, 140
We Bow Down 138
We Gather Together 46
Wesley, Charles 82, 88–96, 98, 99, 109, 111, 140, 150
Wesley, John 41, 88–96, 140, 145, 150
WESTMINSTER 105
We Will Glorify 138
When All My Labors and Trials 130
When All of God's Singers Get Home 132
When I Survey the Wondrous Cross 113
When Jesus Came to Jordan 124
When Jesus Wept 107
Where No One Stands Alone 138
Where Shall My Wondering Soul Begin 91
White, Benjamin Franklin 112
Whitefield, George 37, 93, 98, 99
Whittier, John Greenleaf 135, 159
Whittle, D. W. 128, 129
WINCHESTER 61, 63, 85
WINDSOR 85
Winkworth, Catherine 120
Wonderful Words of Life 128
Wren, Brian 124

Y

Yattendon Hymnal 121
YMCA 127

Z

Zechariah's Song 11
Zinzendorf, Nikolaus von 87, 89, 91
Zion's Harp 110
Zwingli, Ulrich 43, 44, 51, 145